P9-BVM-676

TRAVELS FOR MY COUNTRY

Molly Breene's childhood in a vast rectory in Northern Ireland was good preparation for her later life in the WRNS during the Second World War, and in the Diplomatic Service. Her charmed life included leaving the Royal Naval College, Greenwich shortly before it was bombed, and surviving attacks on Belfast dockyards. Overseas, she survived numerous earthquakes and revolutions, and experienced alarming problems with drunken chauffeurs, a leaking fuel pipe in Bolivia and a truck breakdown in Chile. Here she recounts these and many more adventures from her 25 turbulent years as 'our woman' in so many fascinating places.

TRAVELS FOR MY COUNTRY

TRAVELS FOR MY COUNTRY

by

Molly Breene

Dales Large Print Books
Long Preston, North Yorkshire,
BD23 4ND, England.

British Library Cataloguing in Publication Data.

Breene, Molly
    Travels for my country.

    A catalogue record of this book is
    available from the British Library

    ISBN   1-84262-432-6 pbk

First published in Great Britain 2005 by The Book Guild Ltd.

Published in Large Print 2006 by arrangement with
The Book Guild Ltd.

Dales Large Print is an imprint of Library Magna Books Ltd.

Printed and bound in Great Britain by
T.J. (International) Ltd., Cornwall, PL28 8RW

*For Michael, Peter, Anthony
and Timothy*

CONTENTS

1

Fire, Flood and Fun at Killinchy

I was born in Eastchurch on the Isle of Sheppey, Kent, on 18th July 1919. My father was in camp in the area where a large prison camp now stands. My mother was in digs in a house nearby, not far from the parish church where I was baptised by the Chaplain-General.

At the time of my birth my father had stayed on as a chaplain in the Army following World War I, hoping to remain a regular. However, he did not pass the eyesight test, having had what they called in those days 'a lazy eye' since childhood. As a result of this he had to decide what to do next. I should add here that he had just received the results of his LL.D examinations at Queen's

11

University, Belfast. He had been told he could take the exams but he had better make sure he was successful as it was about to be made an honorary degree and there would be no chance to resit it. Fortunately the question did not arise as he passed with flying colours and was the last person to get the LL.D by examination at Queen's.

I was about to say 'on leaving school' he went into the Civil Service (Customs and Excise) following in his father's footsteps, but then I remembered that neither he nor his two older and two younger brothers went to school – only the two youngest ones (Nicholas and Cyril) went to the Methodist College, Belfast. The older boys were taught privately at home by two brothers called Renshaw known to the boys fondly as 'Fresh Baps' and 'Stale Baps'. They must have been good teachers as all the boys did extremely well, but of course they had individual attention, which must have helped.

My father's first job as a civil servant had not impressed him particularly. He was sent to Londonderry to replace someone who was going on three weeks' leave. When he asked how he should deal with a certain problem, he was told to 'just give them a form and tell them to come back in three weeks'. This he found unsatisfactory. After discussions with his father and the promise of some financial help he started extramural studies at Queen's for his BA, followed by his MA and LL.B. He then managed to extricate himself from the dreaded Civil Service and commenced his theological studies.

In 1912 at aged 26 he was ordained and appointed Curate of the combined parishes of Ballynure and Ballyclare, Co. Antrim. This was where he met my mother, Rebecca Louise Denison. She was then 16 years of age, still at school and studying for her LRAM. She was also the organist at my father's first Watchnight Service at Ballyclare Parish Church. They eventually became engaged, though she was not allowed to wear her engagement ring until she had passed her School Certificate, as it was called in those days. The reason for this was that her aunt (Catherine Aikin) was the headmistress of the school known in Ballyclare as 'Miss Aikin's' – later to become Ballyclare High School.

My father's next appointment was Curate at Glenavy, Co. Antrim, where my brother Arnold was born in 1914 a short time before my father joined the Army. Mother and baby returned to my grandmother in Ballyclare and remained there until Arnold was about two years old. Mother was then packed off to Atholl Crescent in Edinburgh to do a domestic science course (now known as home economics). It was very much the thing to do in those days and the place to go for girls leaving school in preparation for marriage. She had of course married first and was then embarking on the one-year course, which covered household management, cooking, dressmaking etc. By this time my father had been posted to Egypt. On hearing there had been a Zeppelin raid on Edinburgh he immediately sent a telegram saying 'RETURN HOME IMMEDI-ATELY', meaning to Ballyclare and her mother. She therefore went to the head-mistress to explain that she would not be completing the course (she had done nine months of the year). This did not go down very well with the headmistress and she asked, 'On whose instructions are you not completing the course?', to which my mother replied, 'My husband's'. That settled it and she packed her case once more and returned to Northern Ireland.

During his years in the Army (1914–19) my father served in Egypt, India and as a chaplain on board the hospital ship *Olympic* (sister-ship of the *Titanic)* during the evacu-ation of troops from Turkey following the disastrous Gallipoli campaign in 1916, for which he was 'mentioned in despatches'. On demobilisation he returned to Northern Ireland and went to see the bishop who had ordained him. His Lordship asked the pertinent question, 'Where have you been for five years?', to which my father replied,

'I've been a chaplain in the Army.' The kindly bishop then said, 'Well, there is nothing here for you, you should not have gone away. Good day to you!' He returned to England wondering where to turn next.

He applied for and was offered a lectureship at Loughborough Theological College (now a university), but before he got around to accepting the post a telegram arrived from the bishop in Northern Ireland offering him the combined parishes of Killinchy, Kilmood and Tullynakill in Co. Down, at the astronomical stipend of £130 per annum! Admittedly there was a rectory (with 11 rooms in the basement) surrounded by 13 acres of land, of which 10 or so were rented out, by and for the church, to local farmers. The previous rector in Killinchy had 14 children and a wealthy wife so no comparisons could be made there. Each time a new addition to the family came along they appeared to have had another wing added on to the rectory. It has since been demolished and a bungalow built in its place as no-one in this day and age would consider living there. As my father was now a married man with a young wife and two small children the matter had to be seriously considered; however, they eventually decided to accept the bishop's generous offer and return to Northern Ireland.

Early in 1920 we arrived from England and apparently settled in – we had to have two housemaids as one would not stay alone downstairs in the basement kitchen (too scary). I had a young girl as a nanny and we employed a young village lad to look after the garden, but various members of the family seemed to enjoy doing things to it when they came to stay, and my mother was a keen gardener. A man and his wife lived in the large courtyard down below the rectory, where my mother kept hens, ducks etc., and we had a family living in the gate-lodge at the main gate. The cooking was done on oil stoves (three-burner types) and a huge old range, and all lighting was of course by oil lamps, except for my father's rather special Aladdin lamp, which produced a daylight effect that he would write by after everyone else had gone to bed. He would generally retire around 2 a.m. My father wrote for the BBC in the early 1920s and I can remember as a small child having earphones put on me to listen to him read one of his ghost stories. I don't suppose I understood any of it, but I knew it was 'Daddy's voice'. He also wrote regularly for a magazine called *The London Mercury*. There were piles of this large orange-coloured magazine lying around his study for many years in Killinchy; they disappeared when we moved to Belfast to a much smaller house so no room for them there and in any case I think that by that time the *Mercury* had ceased publication.

Following my mother's death in 1957 my father published a book of his poetry in her memory called *Songs of the Nativity and other verses*. These were mainly carols he had written for the parish Christmas card over the years. He would get one of the many artists among his parishioners to produce an appropriate Nativity scene or suitable illustration to blend with his carol.

When I was in India in the WRNS during World War II my father would send me lengthy poems purporting to come from Billy my Cocker Spaniel (a 21st birthday present) telling me how much he missed me, especially on my birthday. I know of course it was really how he himself was feeling about me being at the far ends of the earth. I still have most of these poems in my scrapbook.

A lift was installed from the kitchen to the dining room for food only, otherwise it was cold by the time it was carried upstairs from the kitchen.

The bishop paid us a visit the following year to see how we were getting along. It was like a royal visit – top hat, apron, gaiters, the lot – and of course a luncheon party at the rectory after Morning Service. During his visit he asked my father, 'How much can you make with your writing?' My father replied, 'Around two hundred and fifty pounds per annum', to which the Bishop said, 'Oh well, you ought to be able to live then'; at which point he stepped into his chauffeur-driven car and returned home to his comfortable palace in Belfast. Killinchy is now one of the most expensive and exclusive areas in which to live in Northern Ireland and Whiterock, on the shores of the very beautiful Strangford Lough, has become a great yachting centre.

At about the age of seven my brother shared a governess, Miss Peel, with Tony Raines, whose father Colonel Groves Raines was the local squire. Tony later became well known as the artist of the marvellous big 'Alice in Wonderland' advertisements for Guinness which appeared in the London Underground for some considerable time after World War II.

Alternate months Miss Peel would come to the rectory and Tony would join Arnold for their morning lessons; the following month Arnold would go to 'Ardview', Tony's home about a mile or so away. I presume he either walked or went on the crossbar of my father's bicycle. Eventually both boys outgrew Miss Peel; Tony went to boarding school and Arnold went to a prep school called Lalgar at Knock in Belfast. To get there he had to get a bus at 7.30 a.m. from the village and travel 15 miles. My parents later learnt that things were pretty lively on board the bus, to say the least, especially as from time to time Arnold would produce perhaps a small grass snake, a bat or a mouse to terrify the young girls who were also travelling to their jobs in Belfast. Bob Gibson (the driver-owner of the bus) reported some hair-raising episodes over the years Arnold was a passenger on his bus. Luckily for Bob, it was not for too long as at the age of ten Arnold went as a boarder to Cabin Hill, Knock, the prep school for Campbell College, which he moved on to in due course.

I well remember the day we delivered him there (I was then five years old). We were shown over his classrooms, his dormitory etc.; then he walked us down the long drive to the main road to catch our bus home. We looked back to wave to him and he was raising his new school cap to us. I remember feeling it was the equivalent of going to prison. We returned to Killinchy in a rather sombre mood.

Killinchy was a great place for children and we thoroughly enjoyed it. We had an enormous nursery (required to accommodate the 14 children of the previous rector) so we rattled around a bit in it. I can remember a huge map of the world on one wall and my father lifting me on his shoulders. If I stretched as high as possible I could point out Kamchatka in Russia – a vital piece of information for a five-year-old but I never forgot it. I also remember Arnold and me standing starkers by a huge old-fashioned stove in the nursery while Mother and Grannie Denison anointed us with some kind of yellow cream when we both had chickenpox. We were confined to barracks at the time. Arnold found time hanging heavily on his hands, so he decided to instruct me on certain sections of the Bible but gave up the unequal struggle and reported, 'It's no good, Grannie, she just can't take it in. I'll give her another year and then start her at Genesis.' I think I missed out on the further instruction as I still find Genesis somewhat difficult to comprehend.

The drawing-room was a lovely big room, more like a ballroom, with French windows opening out on to large lawns, the tennis court and, beyond that, the church. The grounds were full of exotic types of rhododendrons which had been brought back from the East by members of the previous rector's family who had presumably made the Grand Tour. There were wonderful trees too, monkey puzzles, eucalyptus, palms and huge trees suitable for climbing (and falling out of, as I know only too well). This all made the perfect setting for the wedding in 1921 of Kathleen Denison, Mother's younger sister, to Dr Harry Hall. I was only two years of age then so I don't remember anything about it, but it was a great family occasion and I imagine all accommodation in the rectory was full to capacity. They were married by Uncle Harry's father, the Rev. T.S. Hall, Rector of Upper Falls on the outskirts of Belfast, assisted by my father. This was followed three years later by the celebration of the 21st birthday of my mother's twin sisters Winifred and Mildred. A charabanc was hired to bring their friends from Ballyclare, Co. Antrim, where they lived, to Killinchy Rectory. No doubt the fun was fast and furious, but again I don't remember much about it as I was probably put to bed early on in the proceedings.

Of course there were no such things in those days as televisions, computers, CD players, digital this, that and the other, for our entertainment. My father was absolutely marvellous in that respect. During the day he would take us out round the fields exploring and looking for hedgehogs, bird's nests, bats, you name it. I had a coat called my 'huntie coat' made by Mother especially for going through hedges and ditches on such occasions. We had a mattress up in a yew tree where we could all go and picnic; even our fox terrier Tip used to join us there. In the evenings (especially the long dark evenings) my father would take his Aladdin lamp and escort us down to the wine cellars – dark, frightening places. Arnold would have a little gun on his shoulder and no doubt I had something equivalent. My father would open the big doors, hold up his lamp and look into the pitch black and say to us, 'Have all these prisoners got plenty of bread and water for the night?' Arnold would salute and assure him they had, and I of course would concur. Then we would move on to the next one. This would fill in at least an hour or so and keep us entertained if not petrified.

One evening while doing our rounds the gardener had brought in a load of turnips or swedes to be stored in the big laundry room in the basement. My father held up his Aladdin lamp and asked, 'Whose skulls are these?' Always anxious to give a quick response, I immediately replied, 'Robinson & Cleavers'. The party collapsed at that stage as my father couldn't stop laughing and wanted to get back upstairs to tell Mother. What I really meant to say was 'Robinson Crusoe's', which he was reading to us at that stage, but I got muddled up with the rather exclusive store in Belfast where Mother and her friends would meet for coffee and shopping from time to time.

We were really fairly normal children compared with nowadays, I think. We didn't get into many scrapes, drink and drugs weren't on the scene then and we were rather limited as to what we could get up to. The only things that left lasting memories were when I set fire to the rectory and Arnold flooded it with 1,500 gallons of our only water supply – otherwise we were quite docile.

To this day I can remember looking at a candlestick on my parents' bedside table and deciding to strike a match and light – not the candle but my father's new waistcoat, which was hanging on the brass knob of the large double bed. This caught light quite well, and then the fire spread to the bed itself. Fortunately the blankets were Army-issue and just smouldered. Meantime, I got a chair and pulled it over to the old-fashioned marble washstand with a huge basin and jug full of water. Unfortunately I could neither see into it nor lift it as I was too small. The next best thing to do was to scarper, which I did making my way down to the basement and closing doors behind me which had never been closed before in our time.

When I got to the kitchen my mother was busy baking for the next church activity, so not wanting to disturb her I just asked for my huntie coat as I fancied a stroll in the garden. However, as I sallied forth I mentioned the fact that there was a bright light in her bedroom on Miss Millar's table (it had recently been bought at an auction in a wealthy parishioner's house). When I had got safely out of the house my mother thought, 'A bright light, there's no sun today, what's she talking about?' She dropped everything and made her way upstairs, opening with difficulty all the doors which I had cleverly shut (to isolate the fire, of course!), to find the bed and bedside table and part of my father's new suit well alight. A firm called Burton's had recently opened a shop in Belfast called 'The Fifty Shilling Tailors' and my father had lashed out and bought himself a three-piece suit, jacket, waistcoat and trousers, for the total sum of two pounds ten shillings. My father always said I never approved of Burton's suits anyway. So I think that was the first and last of its kind as far as he was concerned.

My brother's effort was somewhat different. Father had a marvellous room in the basement which we called 'the wood room'. Here he would saw up small trees on a horse, with the gardener using a cross-saw, to provide us with wood for fires during the winter and it also gave him some exercise. One day Dad, Arnold and I were strolling in the plantation some distance from the rectory when Dad spotted a tree which needed attention. He said, 'Arnold, go up to the wood room and bring me the seven-pound axe – that tree needs cutting down.' Now Arnold was on an exeat weekend from school and was feeling very happy and care-free, so as he came out of the wood room with the heavy axe he took a swipe at the lead pipe leading to our 1,500-gallon tank of water, our only water supply. This was filled by stone-blind Hughie, who came once a week for several hours and whistled hymn tunes while filling the tank to capacity, which he had just done.

As he handed over the axe to my father, Arnold nonchalantly remarked, 'There's a lot of water in the wood room.' My father sounded him out but didn't seem to get anywhere, so we all started back to see what could possibly have caused this unusual happening. My father was not the handiest man with tools of any kind – in fact my mother was the one to deal with anything of that nature. However, time was of the essence and matters had to be taken in hand forthwith. With 1,500 gallons of water spewing out across this huge room full of wood, there was no time to be lost. My father went in with the axe (getting thoroughly drenched as he did so) and hammered up the lead pipe. Arnold and I were given coal shovels and our wellies and told to get on with clearing up all the water immediately. No more exeat treats that weekend I can assure you. As I was not responsible for the calamity, I seem to remember quite enjoying slopping around in my wellies supposedly helping to clear up.

Another little anecdote from the Killinchy days is worth putting on record. My father used to go to Belfast (by bus, of course) from our village – a mile walk up hill and down dale from the rectory. This was in the days when the clergy visited their flocks and many in the bigger parishes in Belfast were unable to get around them. He would do a day's visiting for them once a week to help out. This was a very exciting day for me as he always paid a visit to Woolworth's 3d and 6d store in town and squandered a shilling or two on little celluloid animals (giraffes, lions, tigers etc.). I would be sent down to the gate-lodge at the appropriate time to meet Dad returning from the outside world, and as we walked up the drive he would tell me a story – every now and then he would stop to say, 'What was that noise?', to which I would reply, 'I didn't hear anything.' His reply was usually, 'I distinctly heard a lion roar – it came from that daffodil clump.' We would walk over to examine the situation and sure enough there was a lion! What excitement. Then he would resume his story and again we went through the same ritual, but this time it would be a giraffe he heard in the daffodils. By the time we reached the front door of the rectory I would have collected about half a dozen animals.

One day a very important lady parishioner (Miss Millar of the burning bedside-table fame) was invited to bring her nephew to tea and great preparations were *en train* for the tea party. The nephew was General Sir John Dill, Chief of the Imperial General

Staff (aka CIGS). An ancient lady in the parish had given us a pure white kid as a present but by now it had grown into a magnificent long-haired goat. The same goat would head-butt anyone who came near him except my mother, who of course had ended up with the job of feeding him. He grazed in the long grass under the trees by the drive up to the rectory. On one of his trips to town and his visit to Woolworth's my father had purchased a tin of gold paint and, yes, you've guessed it – the goat's horns were eventually painted gold. What a lovely sight it was – a pure white goat with golden horns grazing in the green grass as our important visitors arrived for tea in their open-roofed Queen Mary-style motor car with the half hood down at the back.

During the tea party the General took my father aside and tentatively raised the question of what he thought he had seen on their approach to the rectory. Miss Millar, his hostess, also raised the question quietly with my mother in case she too had imagined this glorious sight. We often wondered what on earth Sir John must have thought about the Breenes at Killinchy Rectory.

Time to move on from Killinchy days, I feel, but not before I mention that 1924 was a really interesting year in many ways. It was the year of the Empire Exhibition at Wembley. My parents went to it and talked about it for many years to come. To make the journey to London from Northern Ireland then was really quite an undertaking. First of all the bus journey to Belfast with your luggage (no car in those days for them), then the overnight steamer to Liverpool or Heysham, arriving in England around 7 or 8 a.m. to connect with the boat train to London, which took most of the day (and probably still does, I suppose). The journey across the Irish Sea could be memorable, I can assure you, as I did it many times in my youth. The best thing to do was to get your head down and keep it down until reaching landfall next morning. The journey can be treacherous at the best of times.

In January of 1924 the first Labour government came to power – but not for long. It only lasted till November of that year but was noted for having said 'No' to the Channel Tunnel. King George V made his first radio broadcast when declaring the British Empire Exhibition at Wembley open. Its purpose was to strengthen bonds with the mother country and it was described as a family party to which every member of the Empire was invited and at which every part of the Empire was represented. Entrance fee was one shilling and sixpence (7p in today's money). The event was a tremendous success as opposed to the present day Dome experience, so we did get some things right in the 'good old days'.

Another important happening in 1924 was the discovery of the sarcophagus of the boy King Tutankhamen in the Valley of the Kings in Egypt. As archaeology was one of my father's pet subjects, this name was one I had to learn to get my tongue around at a very tender age, along with the aforesaid Kamchatka,

Last but by no means least was the rise in the cost of petrol to the exorbitant price of two shillings a gallon. What an outrage! However, this did not cause an uproar in the Breene household as we did not possess a car. My uncle, being a doctor, was the only one of the family who would be affected by this stringent price rise.

2

Belfast, and the Holiday Rectories

In 1926 my father was appointed to St Peter's Parish, Antrim Road, Belfast. This brought about massive changes in our lives – first of all the move to a small four-bed-roomed town house (rented, not a rectory) where we kept falling over and bumping into everything. I christened the place by falling with my plate of porridge in the first week, which made a big impression on everyone and the ceiling in the dining room. I was really not to blame as I tripped over an electric cable of some sort – no such item in Killinchy Rectory – no electricity! Also a telephone was a new toy for all of us – a sort of wind-up-and-ask-for-your-number variety.

The big moment for me was going to

school, which was conveniently situated almost next door to us. Miss Law, the headmistress, and her two sisters had about 20 to 25 mixed pupils and three or four very good teachers. We received a good grounding in the three Rs, plus English, French, Latin, gymnastics in the winter and swimming in the summer. A two-inch-wide steel ruler which Miss Law always had by her side had a very calming effect on us all. Just the sight of it was enough for most of us to get the message loud and clear. I did not excel in anything in particular, except that I won the Gym Medal, which delighted me but not anyone else as far as I can remember. Miss Law had to come and present it to me in bed as I was recovering from an operation for appendicitis performed by my uncle, Harry Hall, at the Belfast Children's Hospital in Queen's Street in the centre of town – now a police station, I believe.

During the first few years in St Peter's my father's health deteriorated rapidly and I can remember him being brought into the house having collapsed on trams or buses. Fortunately nearly all the drivers and conductors on the Antrim Road route were St Peter's parishioners, so he was always well attended to in times of crisis. Even when he was well they were known to call out 'St Pete's' if he was upstairs with his head in a book and liable to go on to the end of the line. However, it was extremely worrying for my mother and in fact all the family. Eventually a wealthy parishioner insisted a Caribbean cruise was the answer to the problem. A booking was made on an Elder Fyffe's banana boat. These were the main importers of bananas from the Caribbean in the 1920s and 30s. They sailed from Avonmouth to Kingston, Jamaica, through the Panama Canal to Costa Rica, returning via Cartagena (Columbia), San Cristobal (Venezuela) and back to Avonmouth; the whole journey taking about six weeks.

Apparently his basic problem was low blood pressure and all the things he was recommended to eat (e.g. underdone meat, liver etc.) he simply could not digest. While on the cruise he met up with a doctor who said the best thing he could do in this case was to go on a total milk diet for about six weeks when he got home. On their return we all went down to Bangor, Co. Down, to stay with my grandmother and the delivery of milk every day beat all the records for a private residence. My father went on to the milk diet for six weeks as recommended by his friend and spent the holiday walking between Grannie's house and his own parents' home a short distance away in the same road. Eventually he was slowly weaned back on to proper food and by the end of the summer holiday he had made a good recovery, although he remained on a rather bland diet for many years to come. He never touched anything fried and the first thing I learnt to cook was 'steamed fish for Daddy'. When my father was laid low and in bed, my cousin Denise Moffat (née Hall), then about two years old, often came with her parents to visit. On one occasion, peering through the brass bars at the end of his bed, she looked very seriously at him and said, 'Dick – sick.' You could tell then that she was destined for higher things. My father said at the time, 'She has made her first diagnosis.' She had indeed and went on to become a Doctor of Medicine at Queen's, following in her father's footsteps.

Around this time Sir Alan Cobham, the famous English aviator, won the Britannia Trophy for his flight to Australia and back. He also pioneered the 'London to the Cape' route and devised a system for refuelling planes in the air. He moved around the world giving flights to anyone who was brave enough to venture forth in his rather flimsy craft. Amongst those who took the plunge was my mother's aunt (my great-aunt) Sophie Denison, who at that time was a medical missionary with the North African Missionary Society in Fez, Morocco. She had gone out to Morocco in the late 1890s and on arrival there by boat to Tangier found

the final part of the journey had to be completed by camel – quite an undertaking for a
young girl in those days. She was to remain
there for over 50 years and only returned
home to the UK in 1943 due to the fact that
she had gone blind. She was flown home
from Gibraltar by the RAF.

Aunt Sophie was quite an amazing lady.
Not quite the Lady Hester Stanhope, Freya
Stark or Gertrude Bell type, nevertheless she
made her mark on Fez. She was four foot
eleven, a brilliant Arabist and a close friend
of the Sultan of Morocco, whose children
she taught to speak English. She is mentioned in several books on Morocco and one
story I must record was when Aunt Sophie
had invited a close friend to come over from
Tangier to stay with her in Fez. This friend
did more or less the same work in Tangier
and spoke and understood Arabic fluently.
She was lying in bed one morning relaxing
and listening to the crowds downstairs
coming in for medical treatment, and also to
attend a short service (a hymn accompanied

by the harmonium, followed by a few short prayers) before the medical work of the day began. Suddenly to her horror and amazement she heard Aunt Sophie announce in Arabic, 'Will all those with smallpox please put up their hands.' I can well imagine how rapidly she rose from her bed in order to catch the next camel back to Tangier!

The missionaries in those days only came home on furlough every five years and on one of her trips home Aunt Sophie was decorated by King George V, receiving the MBE for her medical work in Fez. She was later awarded the medal of the Order of St John of Jerusalem, which was presented to her by Lady Louis Mountbatten in the Belfast City Hall shortly before she died.

In 1931 we bought our first car – it was an old Essex which looked just like a London taxi and cost ten pounds. Father said we could not afford it but Mother had other ideas, so someone had to learn to drive. As my father was not in the least mechanically minded, he was ruled out straight away. I was too young, which left only Arnold and Mother – he could drive but she could not, so she had to get down to it pretty quickly and under Arnold's tutelage she did quite well. Unfortunately the car kept breaking down and on one particular day we were all out for a drive when it came to a grinding halt somewhere on Bradshaw's Brae (a famous stretch of the Ulster TT course). Arnold got Mother into the driver's seat, Dad and I were posted to the rear to push, and Arnold stayed up front to tell Mother what to do. This seemed to work quite well until Mother let out the clutch as instructed – off went the car in great style and Arnold jumped in beside her, while Dad and I were left to walk about two miles into Newtownards, the nearest town, in the pouring rain. We eventually found them in a garage in the centre of the town and retired to a small café for some refreshments after all our exertions. I really think the people must have wondered about us as we just couldn't stop laughing at the ridiculous situation. Fortunately, the Essex was soon replaced by something with a better engine.

When we were young we used to go to Ramsey on the Isle of Man for a couple of weeks in the summer. We joined our cousins the Bouchers from Donghcloney, Co. Down, where my uncle was the local doctor. My aunt and cousins Bee (later Mrs Peter Palmer) and young Charlie (now Dr C.M. Boucher, retired and living in New Milton, Hants) made up the party. The journey between Belfast and Douglas could be very rough but the trip took only three or four hours. However, we used to enjoy the holiday; the weather always seemed to be lovely and swimming was the main activity for the younger members of the party.

When we reached our teens it became too expensive to go to hotels etc., so my father would take duty in another parish for the month of August while the incumbent went on holiday. We had really wonderful holidays, starting with Ballynahinch Rectory only 15 miles outside Belfast. That particular year my mother had been quite ill with severe rheumatism and the doctors advised an inland holiday well away from the sea. The rectory at Ballynahinch was a lovely big house with a tennis court and croquet lawn, and Arnold and Dad were able to play golf at the Spa a mile or so away. Cousin Charlie Boucher tells me he remembers staying with us in Ballynahinch and walking with Arnold and my father down the middle of the road all the way to the Spa, while my father read something intellectual to them. There could not have been much traffic around in those days, thankfully. That particular rectory has now been converted into a hotel.

The next holiday rectory was Strangford, on the edge of Strangford Lough, Co. Down, with tennis courts and a boat and situated on a nine-hole golf course. I upset the gardener in our first week as I discovered the orchard was full of brand-new golf balls every Sunday evening after the weekend golfers had gone home to Belfast and elsewhere. I was picking them up and supplying Arnold and Dad with them, not realising they were one of the gardener's perks.

The boat was only a small one, but I was the only one who seemed to appreciate it. The Navy must have been in my blood, as I was to discover later in life. However, I was not allowed to go out alone in it as Strangford Lough has extremely strong currents and one could very easily get swept out to sea on the turn of the tide. I always had to have someone with me, and so I devised a plan to take Mary (our maid), who was not particularly keen but could be persuaded with a tuppenny packet of five Woodbine cigarettes. That, of course, had to come out of my shilling pocket money. Anyway, it was well worth it to me, but my father learnt later that the harbour master who lived nearby was quite relieved to see us go home at the end of August without any catastrophes having occurred. He did, however, report to my father that 'the wee girl's the only one who can tie the boat up properly'. That was praise indeed, I thought. I had, of course, used my knotting knowledge acquired during the previous winter months in preparation for my Gold Cords (now called Queen's Guide, I believe).

My father used to hire a gramophone and records from the local village store. We could go down and choose the records – I am sure they were not worth as much by the time we had played them to death over the months we were there, but the shop didn't seem to mind, as far as I can remember. One particular record which we all enjoyed immensely was called 'Minnie the Moucher'. We were all singing it the whole holiday through, it had such a catchy tune. No-one bothered much about what it meant or who 'Smokey Jo', her boyfriend, was. When we got home and found the sexton's wife's dog had had pups and she had reserved the most respectable one (black and white) for the rectory, for which my father gave her half a crown (two shillings and sixpence), needless to say the pup was called 'Smokey Jo' – what else? I discovered many years later that 'Smokey Jo' was apparently a drug addict. We were obviously well ahead of our time and didn't realise it.

The next and last holiday rectory we went to was in Annalong, Co. Down, a small fishing village in the middle of the Mourne Mountains. The sea was on the other side of the road and behind us the magnificent Mournes. Again we had a tennis court and it so happened quite a few of our young friends were down in the same area for the summer. The 'mums' used to get together and organise great picnics for 20 or so of us up in the mountains. We were also near Newcastle, where Slieve Donard (the highest of the Mournes) could be climbed if we felt so inclined. The fishing village Kilkeel was fairly close too, so we were never at a loose end for things to do or places to go to. We had motor treasure hunts, which were quite entertaining, but slightly worrying for our parents from time to time. On one occasion we were told to bring back something unusual. We came back with a 'No Road' sign. My father was horrified and told us to take it back immediately before someone was killed or had an accident.

3

A Passage to India and Other Places

We were still in Annalong when war was declared, and I remember when we got home we were running round the rectory with blankets to cover all the windows to conform with the blackout regulations which had immediately come into force in our absence. Quite a panic really.

Towards the end of September 1939 my parents were celebrating their wedding anniversary and had gone up to the zoo at Bellevue on the outskirts of Belfast to spend the day together. My brother and I were having a cup of tea at home when he was called to the phone. He returned a few minutes later, looking distinctly pale, and said, 'I've been called up and I have to be in the centre of town by six p.m.' He handed me half-a-crown and said, 'Go and fill the car up and go and bring Father and Mother back here as quickly as possible.' He had just returned from Territorial Camp in England and all his gear had to be assembled. I don't know how he dealt with the problem but I expect Alice (our maid at the time) probably came to the rescue. All I knew was I had to get going pretty quickly, even though I had never driven alone before or bought petrol etc., so I jumped in the car clutching my half-crown, bought the petrol and drove out of the town to Bellevue.

Now the zoo is up on a plateau overlooking Belfast Lough with a long winding drive with numerous dangerous 'S' bends. I knew I had to do it come what may, so I got down into a lower gear and just kept going. It was with great relief that I reached the *alti plano*, but at that moment I realised I had no money to get into the zoo and the restaurant where my parents were having lunch. I parked the car and then hung on the wire fencing wondering what to do next, when in the distance I spotted my father's dark hat. I just screamed at the top of my voice and thank heavens they heard me and came scampering out, imagining that the rectory was burning down at the very least. I called them to come quickly and explained that Arnold had been called up and had to be in town at 6 p.m. They came out and the first thing my mother said was, 'How did you get here?' When I told her, 'I drove here,' it was Mother's turn to go pale. She couldn't believe it but then said, 'Well, if you can drive up here, you can drive anywhere.' So that was the beginning of my driving exploits, and I am still driving to this day. I'll probably stop when my licence runs out this time.

I should say at this point that Arnold was first on duty at 6 p.m. on that fateful day and was posted down to Greypoint, near Marino, Co. Down. This was directly opposite the village of Kilroot, Co. Antrim, where there was another garrison also staffed by the Territorials. They formed the protection against unauthorised ships entering Belfast Lough. If a ship entered the Lough without giving the correct signal, the Territorials would open fire. One joke doing the rounds at the time was that Greypoint were informed by one of the coastguards that a particular ship had not given the correct answer on entering the Lough. Greypoint opened fire, missed the offending ship and knocked down a row of houses in Kilroot village. Quite a good story, but I can't vouch for the authenticity of it.

Things moved on fairly rapidly from that point. My father was very quickly back into uniform as he was appointed Chaplain at Victoria Barracks in Belfast. One interesting point to mention is that he was able to wear the same jacket as he had worn in 1919 when he was in the Army, so he only had to have the slacks made. We were all relieved that he did not need his 'putties'. They had been in the attic for years, but one spring-cleaning my mother took the bull by the horns and threw them out (she said they were full of moths!). I don't think my father was too pleased as he felt very attached to them, but Mother won that round, and in any case they were by then out of fashion.

Mother volunteered as an ambulance driver and it was then my turn to join up. I thought as my father and brother were both in the Army, that was obviously where I should end up. Arnold, however, had other ideas for me and recommended I went into the WRNS. I didn't know what they were. I had no idea. To cut a long story short, he obtained the necessary forms for me and explained it was the Women's Royal Naval Service. When the forms arrived I had to sign whether I would be 'Mobile' (go any-where) or 'Immobile' (stay at home). I, of course, was ready to go anywhere, but my father would not agree to that and, as I was under 21 years of age, I had to conform. I eventually reluctantly agreed to go 'Im-mobile' until I was 21 in a couple of years. In any case, it was very early days and when I eventually joined up as a Wren Rating (Signals) we didn't even have uniforms – we just wore a blue armband marked *WRNS.*

The naval base (HQ of the Flag Officer-in-Charge, Belfast) was in the Custom House, near the centre of the town and on the edge of the River Lagan. It wasn't long before we were being bombed fairly regularly. When Jerry couldn't get into Liverpool where convoys assembled before crossing the Atlantic, they would come over to us. After all, they didn't want to go back home fully laden, did they?

The problem for us in Northern Ireland was we had very little protection, and I remember the first raids we had were extremely noisy. We did manage to put up a great barrage of gunfire for the first couple of hours; after that, nothing but bombs and landmines could be heard – we simply did not have the ammunition.

On one occasion we had been extremely busy all evening with 'yellow' warnings on the 6 to 10 p.m. watch. We went off at 10 p.m., had something to eat and then went to our rest room to have a kip before returning again at 2 a.m. We only removed our jackets, skirts and ties, so that if we were called back on watch we could be ready in minutes. After about an hour we were recalled as the yellows had developed into red alerts, and we knew we were for it. We were all immediately transferred underground and work continued more or less uninterrupted. The bombing started and things became extremely lively, to say the least. Harland & Wolff's shipyards were, of course, their main target and they let them have it in no uncertain terms. Fortunately, we currently had three aircraft carriers in port and they put up quite a barrage for us, which helped enormously.

One memorable moment was when a landmine crashed near the Queen's Bridge, hitting the electricity HQ. We actually thought they had got us and I remember getting into a tight clinch with a friend while waiting for the building to come down on top of us. Fortunately, nothing happened except that all the lights went off and we were left in the dark until the emergency lights came on minutes later. It was quite funny to see the Admiral (aka Squeezy Dick) sitting drinking a cup of Bovril and munching cream crackers while dictating signals. Little did he know that at that moment his official car, a Rolls, was a complete write-off and lying on its roof outside the Custom House.

At 5 a.m. we heard the all-clear and came up to find we were practically the only building left standing in the area. Sailors were running with sacks of flour on their backs, trying to save what they could from Rank's flour mills quite close to us, which were rapidly burning down. The whole of the High Street from the Albert Clock to the Junction was on fire and we wondered if any of our relatives could possibly have survived – and presumably they were thinking the same thing.

When it came time to go off watch, we imagined we would have to walk home (five or six miles for some of us). No transport of any kind was operating, of course. We went down to the main entrance and to my amazement there stood my parents – Father with his chaplain's tin hat with the white cross and Mother with her ambulance one. I couldn't believe how they had got there with bomb craters, fires raging and buildings collapsing. My father told me the police and the ARP had all said, 'You go down there, Mrs., at your own risk.'

On the other side of the road was the Dublin Fire Brigade. We just did not have enough fire engines to deal with the situation. Later on, several more were brought over by boat from Glasgow and eventually after some days the fires were extinguished. The centre of Belfast as we knew it had changed completely.

We loaded up the car with Wrens – heaven knows how many there were of us – and my mother bravely drove back through the mayhem again, dropping off people as near to their homes as possible. She really deserved a medal for that, didn't she?

The sailors who trained us were very soon sent off to sea and we took over. Chief Yeoman Proud had been recalled from retirement and he knocked us into shape quite rapidly, checking on everything we did. One of his frequent facetious remarks was, 'Who received this signal – they've got the *Graf Spee* entering Belfast Lough?' (The *Graf Spee* was one of the German pocket battleships which scuttled itself in the Battle of the River Plate in Montevideo.) Then while checking on the map to see where floating mines were being reported he would say, 'This mine is floating down Princes Street, Edinburgh.' We got quite used to it and enjoyed the joke along with him. It never occurred to us to sue him for harassment. He used to say to the head of the watch, 'If the Admiral wants me, tell him I've gone over to Base Accounts.' We of course knew that the Brown Bear pub next door could easily be mistaken for Base Accounts – and it frequently was, I may say. There was a distinct aroma of rum in the Signal Distribution Office when he returned, puffing away on a 'tickler' (hand-rolled Navy cigarette).

Shortly after this the naval base was evacuated to Belfast Castle, which was very convenient for me as it was about 15 minutes' walk from home. Our signal office was in what used to be the ballroom, with a magnificent view over the Lough below us, and I slept two or three nights a week in the castle. We had a marvellous cook, Petty Officer Cochrane (aka Euphie's mum), who looked after us extremely well.

My next step up the ladder was as a cadet when I was posted to Liverpool (Commander-in-Chief Western Approaches), where I went on a cypher course. There were six of us on the course – three passed and three failed and were returned to base. I was very lucky to get through, but just as I was about to leave for the RN College, Greenwich, for my Officers' Training Course, someone developed mumps or measles and I had to fill her place. It was at the time of the

Battle of the Atlantic when the U-boats were hunting in packs and sinking our ships at a rate of knots. I would say that was one of my most nerve-racking moments – having someone standing over you with a stop-watch while you struggled to decipher a signal was not an enjoyable experience. I did, however, realise that every minute counted in these specific circumstances, but I was extremely glad when my colleague returned from sick bay and I was released to go to Greenwich, which I did forthwith.

The Royal Naval College, Greenwich (now a university), was a somewhat overpowering experience for me coming straight from home. Divisions every morning at 9 a.m. and marching everywhere (which up to now I had managed to avoid). I shall never forget the length of that walk across the parade ground to report to the duty officer, 'All present and correct except for...' and then trying to remember the names of those who were not present and correct. This was followed by an hour of non-stop drilling by the Royal Marines when I wore out a pair of naval-issue shoes in two weeks. Then down to work in the classroom with lectures on a variety of subjects, the only ones I can recall were cypher and navigation, of all things.

Meals were served in the Painted Hall and prior to lunch and dinner we collected in the vestibule around the table on which Nelson's body had Lain in State after the Battle of Trafalgar and prior to his interment in St Paul's Cathedral.

What a breath-taking sight it was to walk into this wonderful hall, with its fabulous paintings and long tables laden with silver candelabra, the stewards in their blue and white uniforms (including white gloves) standing on the steps leading up to the Captain's table. Very awe-inspiring I have to say.

A couple of weeks after my departure from Greenwich, the college was subjected to a daylight air raid and the Captain and several naval personnel were killed. I was extremely lucky during the time I was there and never had to go to the shelters once.

On passing out of Greenwich I was posted to Haslemere, in the heart of the Surrey woods. This was a top-secret establishment working on the production of radar for use in the North African campaign, and where all the top brass were known as Captain A, B or C and Commander X, Y or Z. The place was full of boffins, civil servants and naval personnel all housed in a huge country mansion (originally owned by the makers of HP sauce). When an air raid occurred the civilians scattered amongst the rhododendron bushes, but we donned our tin hats and continued with whatever we were doing. To my knowledge, we only had one stray Junkers 88 which seemed to have lost its way home during my year there and as far as I can remember did no harm, but of course it probably took photographs of us.

The only other episode that comes to mind was on an afternoon off duty when I went to the cinema with the naval nursing sister. The cinema was about half a mile outside the town. During the course of the afternoon a damaged Boston bomber trying to return to base a mile or so away crashed on to the cinema and landed on the main road outside. Fortunately, we were in the first row under the balcony and were somehow saved from any injury, but many people were injured, and of course the pilot and crew were killed as the plane caught fire. Not a very nice experience.

I can also remember around this time sitting drinking coffee after lunch on the terrace outside the wardroom overlooking the South Downs and seeing large numbers of planes flying in formation – an unusual sight for us as it was generally dogfights we watched almost daily. We became very excited about this and thought it must be the beginning of the invasion of France, but it was two years too soon for that and we later discovered it was the disastrous Allied commando raid on Dieppe in which so many lives were lost. Apparently the Germans got wind of our plans and were waiting for us.

After a transfer to Newcastle-upon-Tyne I requested a posting overseas and I was offered one of the troop-carrying monsters – the *Queen Mary*, the *Queen Elizabeth*, the *Mauritania*, the *Normandie* and the *Ile-de-France*. However, I decided to forgo the offer as I would not have been able to tell my parents where I was. Shortly afterwards the Director of the WRNS, Dame Vera Laughton-Matthews, came to visit and I made a point of speaking to her at a tea party in the wardroom. A few weeks later I was called to the WRNS Headquarters in London and to my surprise I was told I was bound for India. I had not heard of anyone being posted to India, which was not surprising as we were to be the first to go there, and into the bargain we were to fly.

I went home to Northern Ireland, and while breaking the news to my parents and getting my tropical kit together, I received a telephone call from a school-friend from

Ashleigh House days asking me if I was on embarkation leave. I said I was and we agreed to meet for coffee one morning. It turned out Hilda Gordon, who was stationed in Chatham at the time, had seen my name at WRNS HQ in London and realised we were both heading for India.

We started off together from Northern Ireland and had to stay in London till our travel arrangements were completed. I was billeted at the time in the Golden Square Eye Hospital, behind the Regent Palace Hotel at Piccadilly Circus, which was the WRNS Overseas Drafting HQ. We were supposed to be flying to Lagos, across to Khartoum and on to India and had all the necessary inoculations (yellow fever, cholera etc.) when at the last moment all plans were changed – the plane we were to fly on had been shot down on its return flight from Lagos to UK with the famous film star Leslie Howard on board. The story was they thought Churchill was amongst the passengers.

Eventually one day we were told to report

to the Station Master's Office, King's Cross, at 4 p.m. that afternoon in civvies with hand luggage only. Here we met up with the six others bound for India. We were locked into a first-class carriage with a gentleman who we later discovered was the Queen's Messenger, surrounded by diplomatic bags and presumably on his travels too. We were met at Swindon by British Overseas Airways staff, who proceeded to weigh us and bundle us into a coach, and off we went on a mystery tour of a part of England none of us knew at all. Later that day we arrived in Marlborough, Wilts, and were booked into the Castle and Ball Hotel in the main street. We fondly imagined we were going to spend the night in this very nice hotel and, having enjoyed drinks in the bar followed by a good dinner, our minds turned to thoughts of bed. However, things did not turn out quite like that. At 10 p.m. we were instructed to pack up and get on board the coach once more. We couldn't believe it.

It was a lovely summer evening and we

enjoyed the drive through countryside which none of us recognised. In time darkness fell and we began to wonder exactly what was happening, when we reached the gates of a place guarded by men in uniform with Alsatian dogs. We had no idea where we were and never discovered until much later that we were at RAF Lyneham Airport (Wilts). We spent an hour or so there playing cards and being interviewed by security officers before being bundled into the coach once more. After a drive in the pitch dark we found ourselves alongside a plane, a Liberator bomber, into which we were hauled up by our arms (no such niceties as steps) and by midnight we were thundering down the runway, but as we were totally blacked out and it was so extremely noisy, we could not tell whether we had taken off or not. Eventually a member of the six RAF crew came and spoke to us and informed us there were boxes of food and drink at the back of the plane if we wanted it. Not many of us did, I may say.

We flew out over the Atlantic to the Azores

to avoid the coast of France and by 6 a.m. next morning we were landing in Lisbon, Portugal, which was a neutral country. We, of course, were in civvies and our uniforms safely stowed back in the hold of the Liberator. We arrived at Customs at precisely the same time as a planeload of Germans doing exactly the same as we were – using the neutral country to transport troops.

Our first morning in Lisbon was lovely – bacon and eggs for breakfast, something we had not experienced for several years. Of course we were not supposed to show too much exhilaration over the fact and not to get too excited when a basket of peaches was put down in front of us. It was funny really as everyone knew where we had come from, I am sure.

We got held up in Lisbon for a few days because of sand-storms in North Africa, where we were heading, but we eventually took off and after one or two stops in the desert we arrived in Cairo, where we stayed in the old Shepheard's Hotel, which was wonderful. This no longer exists as it was later blown up during rioting at the time of the Suez crisis.

At this time we got into tropical rig for the first time and I quickly made my way to Army HQ, where I hoped to find my brother. I wandered about aimlessly in this vast building and eventually, quite by chance, I met a rather nice lady who must have thought I looked as if I needed help. She turned out to be Arnold's colonel's wife, and she very kindly got him on the phone and we arranged to meet. He had no idea I was en route to India.

Again we got delayed in Cairo for about ten days, which we thoroughly enjoyed. Lots of friends turned up, including Cliff Holmes, Bill Quekett from Belfast and several others whose names I have forgotten. One night we all went out to the Club de Chasse on the banks of the Nile and enjoyed dinner and dancing till all hours. I must mention here that the young King Farouk was there too, ogling all the girls. When we got back to our hotel around 4 a.m. we found a note on our beds saying: *British Overseas Airways presents its compliments and requests you to have your luggage outside your door by 5 a.m.* We were leaving by flying-boat from the Nile at 6 a.m. en route to Gwalior, a lake in the centre of India, south of Agra.

We made it, fortunately, and I think we all felt a bit the worse for wear for some time till we got used to the frequent ups and downs of travel by flying-boat. The first stop was on the Dead Sea, followed by Habbaniya (Baghdad) and Basra, where we spent the night in the Shalt-al-Arab Hotel. From there we flew down the Persian Gulf (as it was called then) to Bahrain, where we had breakfast in the Malcolm Club. I remember it was around 8 a.m. and we all looked as if we had a bucket of water thrown over us it was so humid. Next stop was Sharjah (United Arab Emirates) and on to Jiwani and Karachi (Pakistan), where we stayed the night. By now we were getting used to the frequent stops when we had to get into small boats and go ashore during the refuelling. On one occasion someone's very nice officer's white felt hat blew off into the muddy waters of the Persian Gulf. Immediately one of the boat's crew dived in and came up with the hat in his teeth and handed it to its owner with a beautiful full set of red teeth marks on the brim. He must have been a beetlenut-chewer, I fear. The hat never recovered.

We made a couple more stops before we reached Gwalior, as far as I can remember, and I believe we stayed the night in Agra before catching a train to Delhi (120 miles north). In Delhi we formed the staff of Admiral Miles (Force C) which prepared the ground for the arrival of Lord Louis Mount-batten as Supreme Allied Commander South East Asia Command towards the end of 1943.

After about 18 months I was posted tempor-arily to Colombo (Ceylon, now Sri Lanka) and made the journey (six days) by train via Madras. I returned to Delhi again by air, this time in a Beechcraft plane flown by a crazy Free Frenchman who flew us into the monsoon. We never expected to reach our destination and I distinctly remember swearing never to fly again, but of course I did many times. I eventually returned to Colombo (C.-in-C. East Indies Station), where I remained to join in the VJ celebrations in September 1945.

About this time, one evening on the 6–10 p.m. watch I went down to the wireless room to check on something. It was always an extremely busy place, as you can imagine. As I passed by one of the W/T operators said, 'Congratulations on your promotion.' I laughed heartily and said something facetious like, 'Chance would be a great thing,' and walked on. Minutes later he gave me the signal which confirmed what he had said – I had reached the dizzy heights of Second Officer and could put up another stripe. Great celebrations all round, of course.

I returned home on the *Queen of Bermuda*,

the first troopship to sail for home after the end of the war. The WRNS went on board in the morning and were well settled in by the time the Army started embarking later in the day. We were standing on deck watching them come on board when I spotted my uncle, who was returning from a tour in Burma with the 14th Army. He had been trying to track me down in Colombo but I was in Trincomalee saying farewell to friends. We had a very entertaining journey home, all packed like sardines, of course, but quite good fun. On arrival at Southampton we found the dockers had gone on strike, so we were unable to disembark. However, I managed to get ashore and phone home but was unable to say when we would arrive in Belfast. After a pretty lively 24 hours on board, which included Scottish dancing until the small hours, we eventually were able to get ashore with the help of my uncle and his fellow officers.

We got on to the train at the docks and someone suggested cups of tea, which we thought was a brilliant idea – except for one officer, who handed a cup to one of the WRNS just as the train jolted and the tea went all over his uniform. On that happy note the train pulled out of Southampton docks and we were on our way home.

After leave I was posted to Londonderry, where we helped in the towing-out and sinking of the captured U-boats in the Atlantic. I would like to have stayed on in the Navy but the men were returning and taking over our jobs again. I was posted to Lee-on-Solent (*HMS Daedalus*) and was looking forward to serving with the Fleet Air Arm, when I was recalled from leave for demobilisation – quite a shock, I can tell you, and something which, of course, could never happen nowadays; but we accepted that sort of thing then and just got on with our lives. We had to – no alternative really.

Looking back over my six years in the Navy, I can really say it was a most interesting period of my life, pretty exciting at times and altogether thoroughly enjoyable.

4

A Minor Revolution, a Bugged Radio and Friendly Elephants

On demobilisation from the Navy in 1946 I returned home to Belfast wondering what to do next. The bottom had more or less fallen out of my world and I was not sure what I wanted to do. I was offered a temporary job in the BBC in Belfast as holiday relief during the summer months. I moved round the various radio producers, taking over as their secretaries went on holiday. As far as I can remember these departments were Talks, Sports, Features and Music.

The Talks producer H.G. Fleet, was very well known in Northern Ireland for his radio gardening programmes. By the time I joined him he had moved on to more varied talks programmes.

When I had undertaken my side of the work H.G. would light up his pipe, settle into a comfortable armchair and read in a very soothing voice what I had typed. I had to check everything very carefully, but I remember it as being a most enjoyable experience working with him.

Another well known producer and writer at that time was Sam Hannah-Bell. One very interesting programme we did was down in the Sperrin Mountains (near Strabane) where we took the recording van to interview and record elderly folk telling Irish fairy stories while we all sat round the open fires in their homes. It was absolutely fascinating. When we returned to Broadcasting House my job was to transcribe the recording – no easy task I have to say as I had great difficulty in understanding their accents. They even used words I had never heard before – probably Gaelic.

I learned later that the programme had been accepted by the 'Third Programme' in

London, which was considered to be somewhat superior to the others at that time. This was quite a feather in the cap of BBC Northern Ireland.

While in the BBC I met up with an old friend who had just been demobilized from the WAAF (Women's Auxiliary Air Force) and during a lunch break one day we decided to go to Switzerland for a couple of weeks' holiday when our spell at the BBC finished. My friend had been at finishing school there before the war, but I had never travelled in that part of the world so it was going to be very interesting for me.

After an enjoyable two weeks in Lucerne during which we travelled around quite a bit, including a trip to Interlaken, Montreux, Lugano and Bern, we met up with some American friends. On our return to Lucerne to prepare for the journey home I received a call from one of the Americans we had met, asking me what I was proposing to do on my return to the UK. I said I didn't really have any immediate plans. He then asked me if I would like a job in the American Legation in Bern – only temporary, of course, as it was the Office of the Foreign Liquidation Commissioner. In other words, disposing of all the excess equipment brought over from the States during the war – mostly small planes and the like. This was too good an opportunity to miss, but I said he must find a job for my friend also, otherwise the deal was off. This worked out quite well and we went home to collect winter clothing, ski equipment etc., and returned to Bern in the autumn.

At the end of about a year there I persuaded my father to come out as Chaplain to the British community in Lucerne for a month. My parents had not had a holiday for the whole of the war years and Switzerland had no shortages of anything as they had hardly been affected by the war. This seemed an excellent idea.

On returning to the UK I did another short spell in the BBC in Belfast before transferring to London. However, I did not stay with them – in fact I never even got started with them in London as I found a much better paid job with Air France, who were just opening up in the Haymarket, London, where I spent four very enjoyable years getting to know London pretty well. Nearly everyone was ex-service, so a good time was had by all.

Around the end of 1951 I began to realise there was not going to be much future with Air France. Jobs were beginning to be filled by French people and young French boys and girls were coming over to work with us to learn English; however, it was not reciprocal. One day I was discussing this with another colleague when my brother called in to see us. He was out for lunch from the Foreign Office. To cut a long story short, he said, 'Why don't you both join the Foreign Office?' This sounded a good idea to us as we both wanted to travel again, so that is exactly what we did.

After my interview at the Foreign Office I

was informed that recruiting had stopped temporarily but I should continue with what I was doing and would eventually hear from them when recruiting recommenced. In the meantime I was called in to the BBC Belfast to replace someone who was ill. While I was there King George VI died suddenly and everything came to a halt, sombre music was transmitted and the recording vans went out in the street to get people's reaction to the sad news. It was a most interesting time to be involved there and kept us all fully occupied, as you can well imagine. A short time after all this an official black-edged envelope arrived for me from the Foreign Office and I was given a date to report to them in London.

At last the day arrived for me to present myself at the FO, and after wandering the corridors of power and mingling with tail-coated brass-buttoned ex-servicemen (several one-armed) delivering files to the myriad of offices, I eventually found myself in the right place at the right time. The first words which greeted me were, 'How soon can you get to Baghdad?' I was amazed at this as I was under the impression I had to spend six months in the Foreign Office before going anywhere. Needless to say, I was delighted and, to cut another long story short, I was on my way to Baghdad within six weeks – in time to hit mid-summer there and 120 degrees of heat for quite some months before it even began to cool down. Shades of New Delhi days when we arrived there in July 1943 to roughly the same temperature.

The journey was quite interesting in that I did not fly to Baghdad but went by Blue Train to Marseilles, where I picked up the French passenger ship *Champolion* (later wrecked off the Lebanese coast in rather mysterious circumstances), which sailed between Marseilles and Beirut via Alexandria. The journey between Beirut and Damascus was by ordinary bullet-shaped coach driven by an Arab (a Yul Brynner lookalike, bald as a coot) who drove like a maniac across the beautiful Beqa'a Valley (the original land of milk and honey) and over the Lebanese mountain roads like a bat out of hell. At times we wondered if we would reach Damascus safely, much less Baghdad.

Once out of Damascus, the journey became the equivalent of a very rough sea journey and it took some considerable time to get used to the crash-bang-wallop movement. After getting my seat adjusted to the sleeping position I was all right and managed to fall asleep – through sheer exhaustion, I suppose. We made one or two stops during the night when there was a lot of noise checking tyres and wheels etc., but by the time dawn came up I felt sufficiently revived to accept a cake-box full of quite good food and a cup of tea or coffee. The Nairn Transport Co. Ltd. (The Overland Desert Mail Service) was started back in 1923 by the two Nairn brothers (Scots) who did the journey in their Cadillac limousine. I imagine it must have been pretty dusty in those days. In 1952 when I travelled there were three classes,

Pullman, second class and tourist class. Pullman was the only air-conditioned one, second class had windows and tourist class had none! The Nairn no longer exists as it was unable to operate during the serious troubles in the Lebanon during the 1970s. Anyway, it was quite an experience.

I spent 18 month on the secretarial staff of the Embassy in Baghdad, which I thoroughly enjoyed. In that space of time we experienced a minor revolution in November 1952, when the Royal Body Guard was sent to protect our embassy on the banks of the Tigris; also a terrific heatwave which killed off quite a number of Iraqis when the temperature soared to over 125 degrees in the shade. At this stage the powers that be agreed to install air-conditioning in our houses, which we greatly appreciated, although we all had boyfriends who had air-conditioned houses, which helped a lot. We had one death among the embassy girls but that was from polio, as far as I can remember, and it was very sudden and very swift.

During 1953 we celebrated two coronations, the first in May was that of the young Iraqi King Feisal II, who had just returned from Harrow public school in England to take over from his uncle who had been acting as Regent in his absence. The second was the coronation of our own Queen Elizabeth II in June of that year. Great jollifications all round and wonderful excuses for new dresses etc. which we all enjoyed.

While writing this I got out my photograph albums to check something. An envelope fell on the floor and I opened it. It was full of newspaper cuttings my parents had sent out to me covering the 1952 revolution. Large headings in the *Daily Express* – 'Down with the British in Baghdad', '20,000 rioters sweep through the streets setting fire to British and American Offices', 'American Embassy blazing' etc. – must have been worrying for our parents to read. In actual fact the best part for us was we couldn't get home across the main bridge as the rioters were busy throwing policemen into the

Tigris and appeared to be in complete control. We just had to spend the night with anyone who offered us a bed. A friend and I spent it with our very handsome Assistant Military Attaché, Tony Parsons, who later joined the Diplomatic Service and became Margaret Thatcher's right-hand advisor on Middle East Affairs. Sadly, he died four or five years ago. I remember when we all met up next morning the main topic of conversation was, 'Who did you spend the night with last night?' It was really very interesting, to say the least. The next day things had calmed down and we all had to return to our own homes.

By the way, the Iraqis did eventually manage to burn down our embassy and the Ambassador's Residence beside it, but I think that was some years later – certainly not during my tour at any rate. Then in 1958 there was a military coup during which they ordered the whole Royal Family out of their beds at 6 a.m. one morning and machine-gunned 30 of them to death. The King was only 23 years of age and engaged to be married to a young Greek girl. They then displayed the bodies of the Regent and others in Rashid Street (the main street) in Baghdad, where they left them for several days hanging from lamp-posts in the intense heat. Photographs appeared in *Time* magazine the following week of the dreadful events. This coup established the Republic of Iraq.

Towards the end of 1953 I left Baghdad for the UK via the Holy Land and spent Christmas in Jerusalem and Bethlehem. This was prior to the terrible troubles which have developed there and I was able to wander around quite freely – the only exception was I was advised not to go to the Church of the Nativity on Christmas Eve as the road from Ramallah to Bethlehem was unsafe due to the drunken drivers. However, I did go early Christmas morning, which was a really wonderful experience.

In 1954 I was posted to Budapest, which was behind the Iron Curtain at that time, so we only did a one-year tour – and that was more than enough, I can assure you. During my tour three legation girls packed up and left to resign or go elsewhere; they were not prepared to spend a year under such circumstances.

On arrival I had a short period with my predecessor before she left to return to the UK. It was sufficient time for me to learn that the housekeeper I was taking over from her was an informer and that I should never bring any mail or any private papers home to my flat. One of my jobs was to take down the BBC European News at 8 a.m. each morning. A car was ready at 8.10 a.m. to get me to the Legation, where I had to have the news on the Minister's desk by 9 a.m. The first thing I did, therefore, was to try to find someone to connect up my radio. My housekeeper said there was a radio shop down below my flat, so I was delighted. She called the man up and he fixed up the nice new radio I had been given as a present before leaving the UK. When I got in the next morning my immediate boss said, 'How did you get your radio set up so quickly?' I told him the man from the shop below my flat had installed it for me. 'Well,' he said, 'you can now take it that your flat is bugged.' Quite a happy thought in one's first week. I felt it was a pity someone had not warned me of that possibility, but I expect that would have been too helpful. Anyway, I learnt the hard way, didn't I?

As my housekeeper made up my bed on the first night, she reserved my blankets, sheets and pillowcases which she wanted when I left in a year's time. At one stage I was off sick for a couple of days and the legation doctor came to see me. Before examining me he said he would like to reserve my radio for himself when I returned to the UK, and so it went on. I paid my housekeeper in tins of Saccone & Speed coffee beans (6s 8d a tin), which she kept in a trunk under her bed. They were more valuable than the Hungarian currency – the forint.

By the time I did leave Budapest I brought practically nothing back home with me. I had to beg my housekeeper not to sell the clothes I was wearing to travel in to anyone who came to the door while I was having a bath in preparation for my journey home. I only just got home before the terrible 1956 Revolt broke out and was suppressed by the USSR. Another lucky escape.

In 1954 my mother's health had deteriorated and by the time I returned from Budapest she was far from well. My next posting was to Beirut (Lebanon), which I was delighted about. It was known as the Paris of the Middle East and, of course, I had got to know it very well during my tour in Baghdad in 1952. I had only done nine months there when I was recalled due to my mother's failing health. I was given a year's unpaid leave from the Foreign Office and returned home to look after her. Sadly she died in January 1957 at only 60 years of age.

In 1956, shortly before my mother's death,

my father was made Dean of Connor. Fortunately, we did not have to move from St Peter's, which was a great relief. He remained there until he retired in 1963. By this time he had remarried and on retirement went to live in Stranmillis on the far side of Belfast. He had lived there as a boy and it was close to Queen's University, where he spent a considerable amount of his spare time. His new wife was known to members of our family and she looked after him very well until his death in 1974 at the age of 88. His Saturday theological article 'From a Study Chair' under the nom de plume of 'Viator' appeared in the *Belfast Newsletter* for three weeks after his death. He always kept them well ahead of the date they were due in case of illness. He had been writing for the *Belfast Newsletter* for close on 40 years and as far as I know had never missed a Saturday article in that time. I have been told that no curate in Northern Ireland wrote his Sunday sermon before reading Dr Breene's Saturday evening article. Quite a good recommendation, isn't it?

When I eventually returned to the Foreign Office after my unpaid leave I was offered Kabul (Afghanistan) or Katmandu (Nepal), both of which I would have loved. However, I felt it was too far away from the UK for my father to be able to visit me or for me to return home urgently if required to do so. The choice then fell to France or Germany, and I chose Germany.

My first posting was to the embassy in Bonn, which we used to call 'the jam factory' as that is exactly what it looked like – a square grey building in the middle of a field a short distance outside the city. It may well be a 'jam factory' now as the embassy has relocated to Berlin, where we have built a rather strange-looking modern building – so peculiar it looks as if it hasn't been completed. We lived in a very nice village, Bad-Godesberg, not far from the embassy, and I enjoyed my job in the Legal Department, dealing with, amongst other things, the release from time to time of the remaining prisoners from Spandau Prison, Berlin, where they had been sent following the Nuremberg Trials at the end of World War II.

After three months I was promoted and moved south to the consulate-general in Stuttgart, which was better placed to explore this very beautiful part of Germany and its surrounding neighbours, Italy, Switzerland and Austria. I bought my first VW Beetle and put it to good use exploring the Alps and the Dolomites quite thoroughly during my three years there. Several members of my family came out and joined me on holidays which we all enjoyed.

My father came out several times to Germany and it was on his last trip he broke the news to me that he was getting married again, which was great news as he was quite lonely rattling around in a large rectory – the sole survivor of the original household of nine. His engagement had in fact been announced in *The Times* on the day of his departure for Germany, which caused quite a stir back home as you can imagine.

On completion of my tour in Germany in 1960, I was posted on relief duties in the Far East. This meant living out of two suitcases for at least a couple of years. One case went ahead unaccompanied to wherever one was posted and the other travelled with you. Quite simple really, as long as you ended up in the same place as the unaccompanied case.

Before leaving the UK I had to take several courses in the Foreign Office, the last one finishing at 4 p.m. on Friday afternoon – and I was flying off at 8 a.m. Monday morning to Hong Kong. I was, I thought, heading for Taiwan (Formosa) and, of course, my unaccompanied case was already on its way there, I thought. I had not been able to collect my passport (due to pressure of work!) so when I phoned the Travel Department to say I was coming over to get it at about 4.30 p.m., they let slip the information that in fact I was not going to Taiwan but Macau. I said, 'My unaccompanied luggage has already

94

gone to Taiwan.' 'Oh no,' they brightly replied, 'it has been intercepted in Hong Kong.' Everyone knew except the person travelling. I then said, 'Well, where is Macau and how do I get there?' 'You fly to Hong Kong as planned and from there you catch the ferry down the South China Sea (three hours approx.) to Macau.' These ferries had British captains with a Macanese crew; they ran three per day and three per night to accommodate the gamblers from Hong Kong. They no longer run, I believe, so I presume there is now an air service. The only plane in my day was a seaplane which flew in laden with gold once a week, which I understand eventually got smuggled back into Hong Kong some way or other (inside the space bar of an innocent looking typewriter or inside an unfortunate chicken).

While in Macau I acted as Pro Consul for nine months and lived in a large flat over the Consulate. I experienced my first typhoon while living there which was quite exciting. I managed to get back from Hong Kong before it hit Macau during the night – I woke up at 3 a.m. to find water pouring on to my bed and my amah trying to sleep on a mat outside my bedroom door as her bedroom was under feet of water. This lasted for two or three days, during which time we could not open our windows or shutters – they had been tied up with rope beforehand. I could communicate by phone with the Consul, who lived at the far side of Macau, but only to compare how many chimney pots or slates we had both lost.

I soon worked out that I could go to a party in the evening in Macau and catch the late-night ferry which would reach Hong Kong by 6 a.m. the following morning, spend the weekend there and return home late Sunday evening. All very convenient and no time wasted. I used to signal to the Consul from the ferry by waving one of the Captain's bath towels to let him know I had returned safely from my travels. His house was in a very commanding position as we turned to enter the Pearl River and the Macau harbour. In fact it had been the Japanese Admiral's residence during their occupation of Hong Kong during World War II.

I should mention here that Macau was a Portuguese colony in those days – a fascinating place for a short spell. You could wander in one part of the town and imagine yourself somewhere in Portugal, then turn the corner and you were in the heart of China with the famous gambling dens open all day and night. It was possible to go out for afternoon tea at the Central Hotel and gamble and drink tea for as long as you liked. Attractive Chinese waitresses dressed in blue uniforms would attend to the tea-drinking side of things, while your gambling requisites were attended to by another lot of young Chinese girls dressed in pale green. The results from the various tables were flashed up on the wall and your winnings (if any) were brought to your table. There was every known type of gambling available and Chinese people thought nothing of spending the whole day or night there. My favourite was fan-tan, which was a pile of what looked like trouser buttons; the croupier would remove the buttons four at a time with a thing resembling a knitting needle. You had to gamble on the number of buttons left when he had eventually worked through the pile. Quite simple for simple minds and it suited me admirably.

Macau had its problems with the number of suicides, mainly brought about by the gamblers coming from Hong Kong. One particular case I recall was of a young lad who was given a sum of money by his parents in Hong Kong to pay off some bills, but instead he took the ferry to Macau and gambled all weekend, hoping to double the money. Needless to say, he lost the lot and rather than go back home to face his parents, he threw himself off the top floor of the Central Hotel in the middle of the day.

While I was in Macau the Chinese multi-millionaire owner of the Central Hotel died and his funeral was more like a carnival. The procession went on for several hours – it started with young flower girls scattering rose petals ahead of the procession, which was followed by masses of enormous paper wreaths mounted on bicycles ridden by young boys. Next came lengths of material in sombre colours carried on large bamboo poles. These were an alternative to sending wreaths.

The encoffining is a very important affair. Friends and relations are invited to the home of the deceased, or in some cases to a large hall, depending on the numbers attending. Then before any action is taken, certain members whose birthdays or ages are considered to be unlucky to the deceased are asked to leave the building. Only then is the body put in the coffin and the procession can proceed. The family surround the coffin, dressed entirely in sackcloth outfits very similar to the Klu Klux Klan. Mourning continues for 40 days after the funeral and a small Chinese string orchestra plays sombre music outside the home of the deceased for the entire period.

After nine months in Macau, I was posted to Bangkok, which I won't dwell on for too long as I did not particularly enjoy the place. I found it vastly overcrowded, noisy and in many ways extremely smelly. Every house had a *klong* in the garden, in other words a stagnant pool or pond in which snakes and mosquitoes bred in their thousands. We all had to take tablets daily against malaria, which was a bore. People picture Thailand with lotus flowers everywhere and beautiful Thai girls in gorgeous Thai silk dresses against a background of a solid gold Buddha. Well, I didn't see many lotus flowers but plenty of bloated bodies of dead dogs floating in the larger tidal *klongs,* which were eventually washed away, thank heavens. Not a pretty sight I have to say.

What I did like was getting away from Bangkok, and this I did as often as possible. One trip I enjoyed immensely was a few days up north in Chiang Mai near the Burmese border. That was really lovely and we were able to watch the worker elephants knocking down trees and piling them up neatly to await removal in trucks. After work they were taken to the lake for 'bath time', which they apparently found great fun. The baby elephants were delightful and full of character; one came and sat down beside me and trumpeted loudly. When I asked the mahout what the problem was, he replied, 'He wants a banana.' Needless to say, I obliged.

Another trip I enjoyed was a tour of the Floating Markets (in Bangkok) at the crack of dawn on New Year's morning. This was fascinating and colourful, though slightly dangerous with so many small boats milling around.

The embassy had two houses down the coast from Bangkok. One was a family house and the other a thatched honeypot two-bedroomed cottage with the sea coming in underneath. We used to get the cook to prepare a large curry and one or two other meals which would last us over a long weekend, so there was no need for cooking, which was nice. A boat would come to the door to pick us up for water-skiing. I can't remember the name of the island but it could be Phuket, where everyone is going nowadays. In our day there were practically no other inhabitants there. This to me was the best part of my posting to Bangkok. By the time I left I didn't want to see another Buddha, reclining or otherwise, in solid gold, silver or any other material. I had had enough and was glad to move on to my next assignment.

I should mention also a most enjoyable trip I made to Rangoon at Easter to spend a week with a friend at the embassy there. I flew on the lovely Orchid Flight, which was sheer luxury from beginning to end. The hostesses wore the most beautiful Thai silk pale lilac-coloured cheongsams (I'm not sure if that is their word as well as the Chinese) and every-thing including the cigarettes was served from Thai silver. Every lady was given an orchid to wear – I can't remember what the men received – but when my friends met me in Rangoon they thought we'd all been to a wedding. It was something I would never forget. The gold-spired Shwe Dagon Pagoda in the centre of Rangoon was fabulous and well worth a visit. I would really have preferred a posting there instead of Bangkok. In many ways it reminded me of Old Delhi.

5

Seoul Survivor

Seoul (South Korea) was my next posting in 1961. My predecessor met me at the airport and, having delivered me to the Banda Hotel in the centre of Seoul, she handed me a bag containing a large slab of chocolate, a detective novel, a bottle of sherry and a torchlight. I did wonder at the time about it but I was extremely glad of all these items as time wore on. The reason I was in the hotel was because the embassy compound was full up at the time. However, I had a rather nice Japanese-style suite there with a large sitting room, bedroom and bathroom en suite.

I had been there roughly a week when I woke up around 3 a.m. one morning, and as it was rather warm I decided to open my window and get a bit more air. It was quite light and I stood at the window for a few moments gazing out at the large square in the centre of the city. Suddenly a shot rang out and I thought how ridiculous to fire at people in broad daylight, presumably because they were breaking the curfew which was in force at the time. What I did not realise was that I was watching the first shots of the 1961 *coup d'état* led by Park Chung Hee, a General in the South Korean Army (later to become President of South Korea in 1963).

What had happened was quite interesting. The Americans had taken the Korean Army up into the hills outside Seoul for 'exercises'. During the night the Koreans managed to disable the Americans, break away at speed and return to Seoul in time to start their dawn coup. I watched the arrival of hundreds of army trucks laden with troops; they all appeared to be heading for our building. I, of course, hadn't the faintest idea about what was going on, but I did think there was a lot of activity in the hotel and it occurred to me that it might possibly be blown up. Anyway there wasn't much I could do about it at that stage. I opened my door and found a six foot six soldier standing guard across it, so I quickly closed it and asked no questions. What I did not know at that moment was they were looking for the Prime Minister, who had been seen entering the hotel, but could not be found. Later I learned that the Americans had smuggled him out down a fire-escape dressed as a nun! No confirmation of that, of course, but it sounds quite feasible to me.

By this time I had retired to the bathroom with some clothes, got dressed pretty rapidly, packed a small suitcase and hoped and prayed someone from the embassy would come to rescue me before the hotel was blown up. What a hope! Eventually I heard English being spoken outside in the passage so I bravely opened my door again, and made contact with some Australians whom I had already met on Sunday at the cathedral. They invited me first of all to go up on the flat roof of the hotel to watch events and later to go down to their rooms for drinks. As I stood on the roof someone called over to me, 'I shouldn't stand there if I were you, the person who stood there in the last revolution was shot,' and they showed me the spot on the railing where they had been hit. I moved on rapidly, needless to say, and we adjourned to someone's room for drinks. As I already had a migraine headache, all I needed was an aspirin and a glass of water.

Downstairs there was utter chaos. However, I managed to get a cup of tea and then said, 'I must get to the embassy.' I walked out into milling crowds and horrendous noise. Planes were dropping leaflets (not bombs, thank goodness), so I started off in the direction of the embassy, which was about a ten-minute walk away on a normal day. I wondered how long it would take on that particular day, or if in fact I would get there at all. I was jostled, pushed, shoved and trampled on, stopping only when I got the chance to pick up a handful of the leaflets presumably explaining what the coup was all about.

I hardly need to tell you I was received with open arms at the embassy. No one had left the compound to find out what was happening and I was therefore in great demand with the Ambassador and the Military Attaché. HE's first words were, 'How did you get here?' to which I replied, 'I walked – and by the way, here are some leaflets which I picked up on the way.' I explained it was a bit crowded and difficult, the Army were firing dummy bullets into the air to keep the crowd under control – otherwise it wasn't too bad. I noticed an old-fashioned glance between HE and the Military Attaché when I got to the bit about the 'dummy bullets'. Afterwards it was explained to me in words of two syllables that they were certainly not dummy bullets but the real McCoy. This was followed by a short briefing from HE telling me I was on no account to leave the embassy compound until further notice unless I was accompanied by someone, and only in transport flying the Union Jack. This worried me somewhat as I thought they might take pot-shots at the flag. However, we sorted it out somehow and I came through unscathed. It was quite an exciting time in South Korea.

I was eventually to travel up to the Demilitarised Zone (the DMZEE, as the Americans called it) between North and South Korea and found it quite fascinating to see psychological warfare at its most entertaining. The Americans were all chosen for their height (no one under six foot six), boots polished and gleaming, uniforms pressed and immaculate. They would take up positions as near as possible to a North Korean soldier who would not be more than about five foot seven and dressed in what looked like plus-fours in which he had slept the night before.

Meetings would take place from time to

time between the North and South Koreans when any problems had to be discussed – like people disappearing or spies being picked up. They met in a long building with doors at either end and the actual DMZ was a white cable down the middle of the table. The journalists of both sides stood outside, looking in through the area where windows would normally have been. The two sides would enter from their own doors at either end and take up their seats directly opposite each other. One story which was doing the rounds while I was there was that a few weeks earlier an urgent meeting had been called, but someone had managed to get in ahead of them and cut an inch or two off all the chairs on the opposition's side, so that when they sat down they found themselves in a very compromising position with their opponents looking down on them, causing tremendous loss of face.

One day shortly after the revolution I was walking home from the embassy to the

Banda Hotel in the centre of the city. To my horror, I came across a young woman lying in the gutter, haemorrhaging – perhaps a miscarriage, who knows? The awful thing was it was the lunch hour and everyone was rushing by and actually stepping over her to cross the road. There was a policeman on point-duty, so I made my way into the middle of the road and more or less dragged him over and pointed to the girl. I then made my way back to the hotel, but I realised the policeman was already back in the centre of the road on point-duty again. I really couldn't go in and eat my lunch thinking about this unfortunate creature, so I asked the hotel if they could help – but no luck there either. In despair, I went to the main entrance of the hotel and quite by chance I bumped into the Australian High Commissioner. I explained the problem to him. He happened to be meeting one of the Army Generals for lunch but he said, 'Leave it with me,' which I agreed to do. At that moment the General arrived in his jeep and off they went. Shortly afterwards an ambulance with a couple of nurses arrived and moved the poor lady to hospital (we hope). I am telling this story as an example of just how cheap life is in the East. I came across this sort of thing several times and found it quite distressing.

My next move was to behind the Bamboo Curtain – Shanghai, of all places. I couldn't believe it. The problem arose because a member of the small local staff at the consulate-general had won some cash – not the Lottery, as it had not started up then, but a Premium Bond prize, I think – and she wanted to join her sister in Japan for a holiday. I therefore had this wonderful opportunity to fill in for her for about six weeks.

I flew back to Hong Kong and travelled by train to Canton, where I spent a night before taking the train to Shanghai. This took about two-and-a-half days – it certainly gave me a great opportunity to see a wonderful part of China. I shared a four-berth sleeper with a

90-year-old lady with bound feet. Her son, a soldier, was also on the train and kept coming to see that she was all right. I brought my own food, though I could have eaten the Chinese food available, but I didn't know about it. A huge wicker-covered thermos flask of hot water was provided for each person and it was changed at every stop.

Life was rather restricted for me in Shanghai and I found I was being photographed quite a lot. I always felt like saying, 'Don't worry, I'm already in the Communists' Rogues Gallery,' having spent a year in Budapest. In the end you get used to it, but I was glad it was only for six week, however.

During a visit of the Chargé d'Affaires in Peking (now Beijing) I came into the office one morning and found a note on my desk telling me to go home and get ready to go on a boat-trip at 11 a.m. that morning. I wondered what was afoot, but soon discovered this was a very unusual opportunity. The Ministry of Foreign Affairs had laid on a boat trip for us on the Haungbu River on which Shanghai is situated. Our Chargé d'Affaire's wife had prepared a picnic lunch for the party, so it was quite an exciting adventure for us all. No-one had been permitted to do anything like this for many years. Of course, our hosts only took us where they wanted us to go and showed us what they wanted us to see. But that was understandable.

There wasn't a lot to do in Shanghai in those days – a foreigner was followed and stared at and so one didn't go shopping or anything like that. I went to the zoo on one occasion with a friend and found the children were more interested in looking at us rather than the animals. I did take up bowling every Sunday morning on the manicured greens of the Hong Kong and Shanghai Bank manager's lovely home. It was an interesting group of people – including a white Russian and a Belgian bank manager who had been interned for several years in Shanghai and had served in the Army in Northern Ireland during World War II. He was married to a

Korean girl, so was interested to talk about Korea when we got the chance. The French Consul-General, who had also been interned for some reason or other, was another member of the group. I have to admit there was more chatting than bowling done, but it was good fun and passed the time quite pleasantly.

When I went out at night, although I took my key, I always found I was locked out when I got back. This was because my amah (maid) had to report who I had been with and who had brought me home. In this connection the chef in the Chargé's house was apparently her boss to whom she had to report my movements. Apparently there was some confusion over this as they did not understand each other's dialects, so heaven knows what eventually got back to HQ about my activities. I would love to have heard the end result. I caused a bit of a sensation at one stage by asking to have my stiletto-heeled court shoes repaired. All that was required was a tiny piece of leather about the size of a

5p piece; however, no leather was available – which explained the excitement my large leather handbag caused when I was out and about.

When I was due to leave Shanghai I had to leave China via Peking – I can't quite remember why, but I was delighted, needless to say. It gave me the opportunity to see many places and things I had only read about. As I was not working there I was able to make trips to the Great Wall, visit the Forbidden City, the Summer Palace, the Ming Tombs and, of course, the Temple of Heaven. Everyone was so anxious for me to see everything and, as luck would have it, I couldn't get a plane out of Peking for over a week. I had the opportunity to return home via the Trans Siberian Railway but declined as I had left personal effects in Hong Kong which I had to collect.

At the same time as I was waiting to fly south, Lady Lamb, widow of Admiral Sir Charles Lamb (one-time equerry to Edward

VIII – later the Duke of Windsor) was also trying to fly south. Some days we would go out to the airport, only to return to the embassy – no planes coming in. Then one day two planes turned up together from Ulan Bator (Mongolia) and a number of very colourful people disembarked. We were able to board immediately – I was on one plane and Lady Lamb on the other. I should mention at this stage these were old Ilyushin – Russian cast-offs, no seat belts and no drinks of any kind except China tea served in large mugs with lids. As I am writing this I now remember the reason no planes had come in was that they could not fly unless the weather was clear – I suppose they would have fallen apart otherwise. Anyway, we stopped halfway in Wuhan, where we all lunched together. I don't recall what we had but it was certainly Chinese food and I remember vividly a great deal of 'slurping' going on; however, a good time was apparently had by all.

On our arrival in Canton a China Travel

representative came on board – at that time they always wanted to know exactly where you had been and where you were going. He had already been on the other plane and greeted Lady Lamb, so when he came on board our plane he called out, 'Lady Breene'. I responded quite calmly and received his full attention and was escorted to the next stage of my journey with great dignity and put on board a train for Hong Kong. All very amusing, of course, and another experience I made the most of, naturally.

6

The New World

I returned to the UK in December 1961 to find the place snow-covered. When I reported to the FO they were somewhat surprised to see me – even wondered where I'd been, it seemed to me. They said, 'We're sorry we haven't got another posting planned for you yet.' I said I didn't particularly mind where it was so long as it was warm. They jumped at that and said, 'Well, we do have something almost immediately in Haiti.' I asked where is it was. 'In the Caribbean,' came the reply. This sounded all right to me and they were delighted at the idea of having found someone willing to go there. I knew it was not one of the 'de luxe' postings by any means – in fact it is one of the poorest countries in the world – but I didn't mind that. I got out my atlas and saw that it was in the West Indies, quite close to Jamaica, and I noted also that it was one third of the island of Hispaniola (the remaining two thirds being the Dominican Republic). The only request I made was that I would appreciate going out by sea and not flying as I had enough of that over the last couple of years. I lived to regret my choice of travel.

Without going into too much lurid detail, suffice it to say we sailed from Tilbury in mid-March 1962 on a small ship called the m.v. *Northern Star*, which was on charter to the Jamaica Banana Producers Steamship Company, and had the worst crossing of the South Atlantic for 27 years – at least that is what the Norwegian Captain told me, and I believed him. The railings on the fo'c'sle were ripped off and crashed back and forth for the ten days we were at sea. There were only eight other passengers on board and I think we all met up for a couple of meals at the beginning and then never saw each other until we sailed into Kingston harbour at the end of our voyage. The Captain came to see me during the voyage and invited me up on the bridge to see the Azores (through a thick mist, I should add) and from that day forth I lay on my bunk and every time the ship rose on a 40-foot wave I genuinely hoped and prayed when we went down again it would be for the last time.

As we sailed into Kingston, Jamaica, the Press came on board and made a beeline for me. I couldn't imagine what all the excitement was about – they asked me where I was going and what I was going to do there, etc. I said I was going to the British Embassy in Port-au-Prince, Haiti, as PA to the Ambassador. 'Oh,' they said, 'the Ambassador has just left on the British Airways plane which flew over a couple of minutes ago – Papa Doc Duvalier has kicked him out.' In diplomatic parlance, Duvalier had made him *persona non grata*. Frankly, at that particular moment I could not have cared less – all I wanted to do was to get on to dry land, find a hotel and go to bed for 24 hours minimum. A car turned up to meet me and took me to my hotel, where I did just that – nothing to eat, nothing to drink – just a bed that didn't roll around day and night. It was then about midday.

At 9 p.m. someone phoned me to say the Governor's Aide-de-Camp had called to see me. I threw on some clothes and went out to find a very handsome young Army officer covered in gold braid waiting for me. He welcomed me to Jamaica and handed me a huge pile of letters for delivery when I eventually reached my destination. They were HE's farewell letters to the Diplomatic Corps in Haiti, which he had not had time to despatch before leaving. Papa Doc had given him just 24 hours to get out. I don't remember what he had done to deserve such treatment, but there didn't need to be a reason if Duvalier was in a bad mood. I had a Haitian friend who had to take a couple of Valium before he went to the Palace just to translate for someone. It really was as bad as that.

With Guantanamo hitting the headlines recently over the transportation of hundreds of 'al-Qaeda' prisoners from Afghanistan, I was reminded of my Haitian tour during the reign of terror under Papa Doc. As if that was not enough to contend with, in 1962 the world was brought to the brink of nuclear war by the Soviet installation of missile bases in Cuba and the subsequent United States blockades. Guantanamo is no distance from the northern tip of Haiti, and as a result we had to make preparations to evacuate all British subjects in the event of war breaking out. *HMS Cavalier* was steaming off the horizon waiting to pick us up if the situation got out of hand. It was an extremely tense time, as you can well imagine. Fortunately for everyone, President Kennedy managed to force Khrushchev to withdraw the nuclear missiles and thankfully the crisis subsided and life returned to normal, or as near to normal as possible in the circumstances.

Another crisis occurred later on, but it was

not quite so alarming. Winston Churchill became ill and everyone thought he was on the way out. We were therefore alerted by the FO to turn up the obituaries we had on him. We searched high and low for any files we had concerning Churchill but nothing could be found. After 48 hours of sheer panic someone happened to see a very dusty box on top of a cupboard marked 'WSC'. The penny dropped that this presumably stood for Winston Spencer Churchill; we got it down and dusted it off, and, sure enough, there were the required obituaries. However, Churchill did not die for another couple of years – 1965 to be exact, by which time we had all left Haiti and someone else would have the same panic stations all over again, no doubt.

While I was in Haiti I had a lovely dog who early one morning jumped on to my bed to keep warm. Annoyed and half awake, I caught him by his collar and pushed him off the bed. As he went down, one of his claws caught my eye and frankly I thought I had lost it. I had to get to the doctor quickly – rather difficult driving with one eye, but it was early on a Sunday morning and there was not much traffic on the road. My doctor's wife, who was an ophthalmic surgeon, got me to her surgery and on examination discovered I had two scratches on either side of my pupil – very painful, I have to say. I ended up with my head bandaged and quite a nasty headache. I was told to go home and rest.

A new Chargé d'Affaires had just arrived and I had to go to a luncheon party at the Residence to introduce various local people to him and his wife. Also Sir John Wedgwood (of Staffordshire pottery fame) had turned up from heaven knows where. After lunch my host and boss asked me to look after Sir John and I made the grave mistake of asking him if there was anything he would particularly like to do. To my absolute horror he said, 'I'd love to see a cockfight.' I had been there a couple of years and had not the slightest inclination whatsoever to see a cockfight. However I found out where there was one and we went. By this time I had a raging migraine headache, so I just closed my eyes and managed to get through the ordeal somehow. I then took Sir John back to my house for tea or drinks and was greatly relieved to find a friend Gerald Carnes, a British priest from the cathedral, awaiting our return. I have never been so glad to see anyone. My eye made a good recovery but it was a nasty experience. To damage one's eye is bad enough, but to have to go to a cockfight into the bargain is just too much.

Tragically the year 2004 has produced one of the worst disasters ever to hit the Republic of Haiti in the Caribbean. The tropical storm Jeanne approached the area during a night in mid-September completely devastating much of the country and in particular the area around the northern city of Gonaives.

Most of the flimsy houses stood no chance against the force of the hurricane. So far the death toll is reported to be around 2,000, but many hundreds are still unaccounted for having been swept out to sea. Over 300,000 are said to be homeless and starving and the situation is still reported as being critical.

Those who are left to pick up the pieces will require a tremendous amount of help and support to get them back on their feet again. Let us hope and pray they will get it.

After a year in the Foreign and Commonwealth Office (as it had become by then) I was posted to La Paz (Bolivia) in 1966 as Vice Consul. There were no direct flights to Bolivia at that time so I had to fly via New York and Lima (Peru). This gave me the opportunity to meet up again with Al Voegeli, the Bishop of Haiti, who, since we last met, had been expelled at gunpoint from Haiti by Papa Doc Duvalier. After an enjoyable weekend Al took me to the airport and, finding all parking spaces full, he dropped me off and I proceeded to check in. This proved to be quite difficult but I eventually managed it. However, I realised things were not going according to plan somehow – it was even difficult to find somewhere to stand much less sit. After some time a British Airways official came and sought me out and informed me there was going to be a long delay; he escorted me to the Monarch Lounge (BA's first-class waiting area) where I learnt for the first time ever New York air traffic had ground to a complete halt – nothing (repeat nothing) was moving in or out of New York. I spent quite a long time there; I can't recall exactly how long, but enough time to eat, sleep, write letters and post them all at British Airways' expense.

When things eventually got moving again, we boarded the plane for Lima and started to move off. All one could see were lines of planes head-to-tail moving very slowly. At that stage I began to wonder whether we would get safely off the ground, never mind make it once we all got in the air. Not the best situation for starting off on a long-haul journey.

On arrival in Lima I asked about the once-daily flights to La Paz, but discovered the passengers had already boarded. Meantime I found out there had been an oil leak in our hold and some of the baggage had been destroyed. Miraculously, mine had escaped damage and I was able to retrieve it and make my way to the next stage of my journey. I saw the Lloyd Aero Boliviano plane was still being loaded – I was not impressed. It looked as if it had been on fire at some stage and appeared to me like something left over from the First World War. However, I fought my way on board and we eventually took off and settled into our bucket seats to admire the view as we flew over what looked like dense jungle. It occurred to me that if we came down there would be very little chance of ever being rescued. As I was looking into the distance from my window, I realised we were approaching a volcano, so I quickly beckoned to an American girl wielding a camera opposite me. 'Come over here with your camera,' I said. 'We're coming close to a volcano – extinct, I hope.' As we came level with the volcano the pilot tipped up the wing and we were able to look straight into the crater, which was smouldering and full of sulphurous-looking material. It was far from extinct.

We arrived some hours later, having tipped up and looked into several more volcanoes – in fact I was becoming quite blasé about them by the time we started our descent to fly low over Lake Titicaca (the highest large lake in the world) before landing in La Paz. There I made my way to the airport lounge and settled down to await someone from the embassy to meet me. I waited quite a while, but I was not going to move anywhere as I found my hand-luggage had suddenly become rather heavy. We had landed on the *alti plano* at La Paz at 14,500 feet (the highest commercial capital in the world).

After a while one of the embassy girls

arrived and asked me if I had been there long. She told me she had been waiting for me to come in on the Braniff plane. We are not supposed to fly Lloyd Aero Boliviano – they are inclined to fall into the volcanoes between here and Lima. I had made my first and last trip with them.

It was during my time in La Paz that Che Guevara, the Cuban Communist revolutionary, was blazing a trail through Bolivia. He was hunted down and executed by the Bolivian Army, which provided us with quite a bit of excitement at the time.

I understand the Americans are currently starting a revolution of their own in Bolivia by trying to eradicate the growing of coca – the symbol of the Inca nation. It is grown all over Bolivia (as we grow wheat). They have four harvests a year. It is sold in their markets and used in the production of cocaine for the narcotics trade. The country is already in dire economic straights, so it is no wonder the Americans are not having much success in eradicating it so far. I don't know what they suggest as a suitable financial substitute for it. As everyone chews coca leaves, I wondered if chewing gum would do.

On one occasion I was giving a supper party for about 30 friends. Early in the evening, while guests were arriving in dribs and drabs, I went into the guest bedroom to get extra chairs. To my horror I found our accountant lying on one of the unmade-up beds, bright red in the face and clutching the bed-head, apparently in great pain. I immediately thought he was suffering from appendicitis. I had invited the embassy doctor, who lived nearby, so I sent someone to get him to come as soon as possible. I got the patient into my own bedroom and settled him down on my bed. The doctor arrived quite soon afterwards and quickly diagnosed it was an attack of gallstones, which of course can be extremely painful. As we stood round the bed my Indian maid came in and joined us. The doctor asked me if I had any coca leaves in the house and I immediately told him I certainly did not. He then spoke in Spanish to my maid, who trotted off into the kitchen and in no time was back with a large pot of coca-leaf tea. Apparently my flat was full of it. The patient drank a cup of the concoction and went out like a light. The party continued until one or two in the morning and I was beginning to wonder where I was going to sleep as it was proving difficult to wake the patient. However, with the help of his very pregnant wife we managed to get him on his feet and on his way. The result of all that was that he was flown home to the UK for surgery and I took over his job as Accountant as well as my own two jobs of Vice Consul and Administration Officer.

The Administration Officer's job with the embassy was a very varied one. It covered just about everything imaginable, but the job I am going to tell you about now was rather unusual, to say the least. The Head of Chancery and his wife, good friends of mine, had been transferred to Santiago (Chile) as David (an ex-Guards officer) could no longer physically survive in La Paz. He had suffered a bad bout of polio in Egypt and nearly died. As a result, his walking was impaired and he had great difficulty in getting around. I remember my father telling me about a parishioner who had returned from South America and saying, 'In La Paz you either walk or talk, but you can't do both.' Well, David just had to be moved down to sea level if he was to survive.

The problem was they had a dearly-loved boxer dog called Barney who had to be shipped down to them in Santiago, and the job fell to me to undertake the necessary steps and see that no harm came to him en route. Fortunately I am an animal lover, so I was determined Barney would make the journey as quickly and comfortably as possible.

The first thing I had to do was have a large box made by the embassy carpenter with plenty of air holes so that he did not suffocate and also big enough so that he would not feel too cramped. I took him to the airline office to have him weighed, and the minute the Indian staff saw him they all disappeared underneath the counter. I had therefore to get Barney on to the huge slippery scales myself, and get him to 'sit and stay' without falling off, while the staff very gingerly re-appeared and recorded his weight.

The day came when Barney was to make his big journey. The embassy car collected us to take us to the airport; the container had already been delivered, so when we arrived all I had to do was track it down, check him in, and take Barney, already kitted out in his new hand-knitted emerald green polo-necked sweater, for a brisk walk before getting him loaded on to the plane. As we walked, I noticed a large army barracks on my right and on the wall I saw what I thought was a stone figure of a large eagle-like bird. When we approached, to my amazement the stone figure suddenly came to life and swooped down in our direction and ran along the road – wings outstretched. Presumably it was more interested in Barney than me, but he couldn't have cared less and was totally unaware of the danger he was in. The bird turned out to be a condor, the biggest as well as the heaviest bird that flies, with a wingspan of approximately nine feet. It was the mascot of the Bolivian Army and some soldiers from the barracks came running out to rescue it (not us). They retrieved it in the nick of time – and we made for the airport at the double!

I accompanied Barney out to the aircraft and saw him safely loaded, making sure the air holes were not covered up. He had to change planes at Lima, but the next day I got a phone-call from David to say he had arrived safely. What a relief!

7

Two Car Stories – and Two Vice Consuls

In the spring of my first year in Bolivia, three embassy friends and I decided we would go to Oruro for the annual carnival. We started off between 1 and 2 p.m. in my new Austin 1100 and had booked in to a convent in Oruro, where we hoped to arrive around 6 p.m.

This journey was a bit tricky: you had to be sure to fill up your petrol tank at a certain point as it was the last one before Oruro. All went well, we filled up at the appropriate place and were quite happy that we had remembered our instructions. However, as we continued our journey I noticed my petrol was disappearing rather too rapidly for my liking. Eventually around 3 p.m. we had to stop and pull off the road and ponder what to do next. There was not a lot of traffic on this road, so I realised I had to take action pretty quickly before it started to get dark. We had just passed a memorial on the side of the road to a party of six people who had been bumped off some years back at exactly the same spot, probably stranded like us. Not a happy thought.

I got my heavy white sweater out of the boot of the car and when I saw the next vehicle approaching (there were not many) I stood in the middle of the road waving it frantically. I asked the driver to send out a breakdown truck to help us, but nothing arrived. Soon afterwards a Land Rover came along with two men. The driver, who was English, got out and did a sort of Walter Raleigh act – threw his jacket on the ground, crawled underneath and informed us a screw was missing from the petrol tank. After some discussion he stepped out and stopped the next truck, which had a couple of Indian women (complete with bowler hat and pigtails) in the back apparently going home after a hard day's work in the fields. He instructed them to go back to the last village, buy a bar of Sunlight soap and a bag of sugar and return as quickly as possible. The women began to cry, but no one took any notice and in half an hour they returned with the necessary items. Our friend instructed the two women to mix up the soap and sugar in a dish, which they did, still crying as they worked. Eventually the man took the concoction, rolled a lump of it in his hands, crawled under my car, shoved it into the hole in the petrol tank to replace the missing screw and said, 'Now pray!'

Our friend departed and we also got under way. By this time it was getting dark and we still had about 56 miles to go. We eventually arrived in Oruro, but too late for the convent where we were booked to stay – they had all gone to bed hours before. We therefore spent the night in the car, but by this time the petrol was beginning to drip out of the tank.

There were quite a number of drunks already in the carnival spirit wandering around aimlessly and I was worried in case someone would throw down a cigarette and we would all go up in flames. I therefore walked the streets wrapped in a blanket (it was very cold) and kept guard while the others tried to sleep and we all patiently waited for daylight. We hoped that a priest would arrive at an early hour for Mass at the convent, where we had parked outside the main gates. I remember saying, 'Good morning, Father?' in several languages to everyone who passed by, and at last we were in luck. The door opened at about 6 a.m. and we managed to creep in behind Father. What a night!

The car was repaired in no time and we saw the carnival, but strangely enough I don't remember much about it. The return journey was uneventful, but I soon realised the missing screw had been cleverly loosened prior to our journey and the embassy driver was the culprit. This made me even more determined than before to see him on his way, but his luck was beginning to run out in other directions as well.

One day the Head of Chancery was accosted outside his house by a woman shedding copious tears – she told him that every time the Ambassador had a delivery of liquor from the UK her husband – our driver – was not sober for several weeks on end; eventually that did the trick and he had to go, but not before we paid him a vast sum of money (severance pay) as he had been with the embassy for so many years. I expect his wife was delighted.

Around this time we were due to change ambassadors, and after numerous farewell parties for the outgoing ambassador we were all in a rather fragile state. I had been working overtime with the portable oxygen which I had to keep ready in my flat over the embassy, or in the back of my car when going to the airport to meet the Queen's Messenger, or of course for fragile ambassadors celebrating their departure from La Paz.

A new Rolls Royce which had been ordered

for the Ambassador had arrived and the old one was ready to be shipped back to England. We had considered selling it locally and very quickly found a buyer, only to discover the man who was buying it wanted to use it as a mobile brothel. The outgoing ambassador was, needless to say, deeply shocked and instructed it should be returned to the UK immediately.

When the day came for HE's departure we all went to the airport to see him off and returned home utterly exhausted. I decided to have a hot bath and go to bed early – the first early night for weeks. I was just about to put my foot into the bath when I was called to the phone. It was a British Subject ringing to say he had been driving home down in the valley and wondered what the Ambassador's new Rolls was doing parked in a peculiar position in the dark and apparently no one in it. That was the end of my early night.

I rang one of the Second Secretaries and said, 'What are you doing at the moment?'

He replied, 'I'm just going out to a party.' I said, 'No you aren't, you are coming with me to find out what has happened to the new Rolls.' He agreed, and came and picked me up at the embassy.

We drove out of town and down into the valley in the direction we had been given, only to find HE's driver drunk in the front and a huge dent in one of the mudguards. The driver was, of course, removed by the police. We tried to move the Rolls but could not budge it as the mudguard was pushed on to the wheel, so we had to call for the break-down-gang to come and get it. By 1 a.m. we had been joined by several members of the British community who just happened to be passing by and we formed quite a procession up into La Paz, where we left the Rolls to be repaired in a garage.

It transpired that the driver had returned from the airport after seeing the Ambassador off and went to the Residence, where he helped the staff see off any left-over drink. Apparently there was enough for them to thoroughly enjoy themselves as it took about 24 hours for him to come round and realise where he was – in gaol! He was also sacked, of course.

The problem then arose – what to do with the damaged Rolls? The new ambassador was due shortly and it must be in spanking condition for his arrival. Suddenly it occurred to the Head of Chancery that the old Rolls had not become a mobile brothel, but was languishing in a garage in town waiting to be shipped back to the UK. We quickly ordered the front mudguard to be removed from the old Rolls and replaced it with the damaged one from the new one. After re-spraying to match, the Rolls looked as good as new and we all breathed a sigh of relief once more.

In 1968 I was transferred to Guatemala, and on the day I was told about it the United States Naval Attaché was shot dead while walking in the main street. This hit the headlines, so I was a bit worried about telling my father where I was off to. However, he had to know eventually, of course.

I left La Paz with a friend, an ex-Benenden girl who had been staying with me and whose father had been the head of the railways in Bolivia. She was heading for Houston, Texas. We flew directly to Panama, where we stayed one night. I would then go on to Guatemala on the flight known to the locals as 'the milk run', which stopped en route in almost every capital city in Central America, ending up in Mexico City. My friend would continue her journey in the other direction to Houston, Texas.

The first night in Panama I found I could not breathe properly when I lay down, so I sat up all night and dozed. Next morning I called in to our consulate to see about my visa or whatever was required to get into Guatemala. During our conversation the Vice Consul suggested I should see the embassy doctor as by this time I could scarcely talk. I went to see the doctor and as I walked into his surgery he said, 'How long have you suffered with asthma?'

I told him I had never suffered with it in my life. 'I was quite all right when I left La Paz yesterday morning,' I said.

He looked at me in amazement and said, 'Have you any idea what height Panama is above sea-level?'

I admitted I had not the slightest idea. He then informed me it was 50 feet above sea level and that coming down from 14,500 feet to 50 feet above sea level in one day had affected my lungs. I was about a month recovering.

I was met at the airport by a rather prosperous-looking middle-aged man driving a large car. He asked me what I was going to do in Guatemala. I said, 'I'm replacing the Vice Consul,' to which he replied, 'I'm the Vice Consul and I'm not going anywhere.' I did not argue the point with him and just decided to go along with whatever worked out – after all, I had nearly burst my lungs in my effort to get there.

I lived in a nice local hotel in the centre of

the city and decided to work on my Spanish by listening to the news every day and anything else of interest I could find on the radio. One morning I put on the radio by my bed as usual and lay there listening to what I thought was a repetition of John F. Kennedy's assassination. I thought it was rather odd, and as I listened more attentively I heard them mentioning Robert Kennedy's name. I was in fact listening to the report of Robert Kennedy's assassination. I couldn't believe it and frankly thought I must have misunderstood what they were saying, so I did not say a word to anyone in case of being accused of scaremongering. I went down to breakfast and as the head waiter was the only one who spoke English in the hotel, I called him over and quietly asked him about what I thought I had heard. He went off and in a few minutes returned to confirm that Robert Kennedy had indeed been assassinated. I remember walking to the consulate that morning carrying my little radio and listening to the news, which was coming in all the time with more details of the tragic event.

I enjoyed travelling around Guatemala very much indeed and visiting lovely colourful Indian villages up-country with names like Chichicastananga (pronounced 'Cheecheecastananga'). It seemed to me that everyone had a volcano in their back garden; a member of staff even asked me if I would like to climb one – I declined the invitation, needless to say. It would just have been my luck for it to erupt the day I climbed it, I felt certain. The point was, it was not only eruption one had to watch out for, but following heavy rain the craters filled up and the rim would give way, sending rivers of thick mud down which covered the surrounding district. All very fertile, of course, so all the locals rushed to set up home in the area. I couldn't understand that at all.

After about six weeks a telegram arrived one day from the FCO saying, 'Miss Breene should proceed immediately to … (corrupt group). She should arrive there by … (another corrupt group)' and so it went on. It was quite a long spiel, but eventually by a process of elimination we deduced that it must be Chile I was to proceed to and I was to go there to assist with the Queen's forthcoming visit in two or three months' time.

Before leaving Guatemala for Chile I took a few days' leave and flew to Mexico, where I spent the time sightseeing. One of the interesting places I went to was the big new university. Shortly afterwards I heard it had been completely destroyed in a terrible earthquake. Another lucky escape for me.

I was to fly Air Canada to Lima and then up to La Paz (by Braniff) and eventually on to Santiago, Chile. I had dinner in my hotel in Mexico City and then made my way to the airport. We got as far as boarding the plane around about 8 p.m. and sat there for some considerable time. We then disembarked and went back to the terminal, where we were offered a free meal – which I, of course, did not want as I had just had dinner.

As I looked around my travelling companions it seemed to me that out of the 70 or 80 people (or perhaps more), mostly short, stocky, swarthy Mexicans, there was only one good-looking fellow amongst them – a tall, blond, handsome character who really stood out from the rest. About 10.30 or thereabouts we boarded our plane once again and there we sat on the tarmac until midnight. By this time I was hopping mad because I had to catch a plane in Lima for La Paz – one flight daily, as before. I wondered if by any chance the Bolivian flight might be delayed, so when we eventually reached Lima I made sure I was first in the queue to get off and made a mad dash for the check-in desk (Braniff – not Lloyd Aero Boliviano). Needless to say, the plane had just departed – I was furious and told Air Canada that I would now have to spend 24 hours in Lima before getting my plane to La Paz. I told them in no uncertain terms that I expected them to put me up in a hotel at their expense etc. They listened quite politely to my tirade and said they would do just that.

After a few minutes the hostess returned and handed me a voucher for 'a double room' in the Gran Bolivar Hotel (the best hotel in Lima in those days). I queried the 'double room' as I felt it was a bit unnecessary, but the hostess replied very nicely that 'it is for you and your husband'. I looked to see who she thought was my husband, and there standing right behind me was the gorgeous blond creature. We all burst out laughing and I had to confess he didn't belong to me. It certainly broke the ice, which was nice, and we shared a taxi up into town. He was a Yugoslav married to a Brazilian and was (like me) trying to make a connection, not to La Paz but to Rio de Janeiro. I checked in at my hotel and we arranged to have breakfast and lunch together and even did a tour of Lima – something I had always wanted to do – before he disappeared out of my life to join his wife in Rio.

8

A Chile Reception

I arrived in Santiago, Chile, well ahead of the Queen and the Duke of Edinburgh and after some time found myself a flat as I expected to be there for at least three or four months. I had heard through the grapevine of a flat which was going to be available for about that length of time and this suited me very nicely. I moved in as soon as possible.

This flat was rather grand, with chandeliers in every room, masses of very valuable ornaments everywhere and monogrammed sheets etc. I very soon realised that the chandeliers were a marvellous warning of impending earthquakes. I would wake up at the first tinkle of the chandeliers but I didn't bother to get up until the wardrobe doors started to clatter. At that stage I went round the flat at the double, placing all the valuable ornaments at ground level. I did notice that quite a few of them had already suffered some damage; however, I was not prepared to take any risks.

During my first week or so I was quite busy at the embassy and had not had time to meet any of my neighbours in the flats roundabout. Then one evening around 9 or 10 p.m. I received a phone call from one of them. She was surprised to hear there was a stranger in their midst but told me she would like to meet me and invited me to one of her weekly drinks parties, which I appreciated. She also advised me to keep my door locked as there seemed to be rather a lot of activity out on the staircase, which I was unaware of till that moment. When I examined my door I discovered the lock was far from safe, something I had not noticed before. I therefore checked to see what all the fuss was about and saw a number of men sitting on the stairs down below (I was on the top floor). I went inside again and put a chair under the door handle and went to bed. I gathered later that the area left a lot to be desired in more ways than one and I made plans to move elsewhere as soon as possible.

Before 'The Visit' I moved to a flat belonging to a Chilean general who was going to the United States for a spell. It was in the equivalent of our Whitehall area and very convenient for the embassy. I also took over his maid, who looked after me wonderfully and helped me in numerous ways. One night after a cocktail party at one of the embassies I brought a couple of colleagues back to my flat for a nightcap and we discussed the forthcoming 'Visit' and one thing and another. One of them had been in the Navy and so we had to compare postings etc. Suddenly someone said, 'What is that strange bright light appearing over there?' To cut a long story short, it was the dawn coming up – we had in fact talked all night. Fortunately, it was a weekend so no real harm was done.

As time went on, preparations were almost complete for the arrival of the royal visitors. They were to stay in a large and spacious palace in the centre of Santiago (Indira Gandhi having been the last visitor to stay there some months before). Their programme had been meticulously worked out for the three-to-four-day visit and printed in a small booklet which had been distributed to all those concerned with the precise timings of their movements. They were due to arrive on the following Monday around midday. On Saturday evening everyone was glued to their television to see the evening news when, horror of horrors, we saw pictures of the palace where the Royals were supposed to be staying going up in flames. Briefly, while the electricians were installing a plug for the Duke of Edinburgh's electric razor, something went seriously wrong causing the fire. Panic stations all round!

The result was we had to take the 14th and 15th floors of the Hilton Hotel for the Royal party. Everything had to be provided by the British community and we had only 24 hours to get it all together. The whole programme had to be re-planned, but it went ahead and towards the end we all had to attend a reception at the Residence. We got out all our glad rags and it was explained that we would only be presented to either Her Majesty or the Duke of Edinburgh but definitely not both. We stood round in a semi-circle in the drawing room of the Residence and waited. The Queen was to go down one side and the Duke the other, however, as he is wont to do, the Duke followed Her Majesty and the end result was we were all presented to both of them. The men all wore their regimental ties, which proved a great talking point for the Duke as he recognised them all.

I had bought rather a nice white sleeveless dress with an embroidered panel down the front while I was in Guatemala, with no thought of a Royal Visit in mind. I had passed it in a shop window every day walking to the consulate, and one day I just popped in and bought it. I had not worn it, so when I heard of my posting to Chile I put it aside and decided it would be quite suitable for the occasion. I had no hat or shoes but left that to deal with in Santiago when I got there. On arrival I discovered everyone seemed to be flying over to Buenos Aires to buy their outfits, as there was very little available in the shops in Santiago.

I decided I would probably find the right shoes, but had given up on the hat problem until I spent a weekend with my friends from La Paz days (the owners of Barney the boxer dog I helped to join them from La Paz). They had just spent a year or two in the Protocol Department in London and had had to attend functions in Buckingham Palace, Ascot etc. As a result my friend had a small room full of glamorous hats. She took me in and said, 'Help yourself.' I couldn't believe my luck. I picked out a gorgeous frothy, chiffon number in various shades of pink, which was just the thing for the occasion. My friend then said, 'Now take that home and hang it up in the bathroom when you have a bath. The steam will soften it up and you can then fix it to suit yourself.' I was thrilled. I managed to find a nice pair of shoes and matching handbag, plus the inevitable three-quarter-length white gloves. When Her Majesty appeared, horror of horrors, our outfits were very similar – her hat was slightly paler than mine – causing quite a bit of amusement among my pals. I expect her outfit cost slightly more than mine, however. I did wonder if I might get sent to the Tower for such an indiscretion.

The most unforgettable part of the visit was saying farewell to the Royal Party on board the Royal Yacht, which was to take them to the next port of call. It was around 8 or 9 p.m. and the whole place was floodlit. The Marines Beat the Retreat on the dockside, ending with 'Oft in the Stilly Night' and 'Sunset', which are guaranteed to reduce everyone to a pulp. Then the Royal party appeared on deck in evening dress and tiaras to wave farewell to everyone, and we watched as the Royal Yacht pulled gently away into the night. It really was a glorious sight.

I was fortunate enough to accompany the Foreign Office inspector and his PA down to Valparaiso to close down the consulate, which had been open since the days of sailing ships. The captains came ashore and placed their ship's papers in the consulate for safe keeping while they loaded or unloaded their cargoes. In those days it was really dangerous coming ashore in foreign countries where they could be, and frequently were, press-ganged and the ship's papers stolen.

We had been back only a short time when Valparaiso was devastated by a severe earthquake, which we got the edge of in Santiago. It was then that I learned there were at least two kinds of earthquakes – vertical and un-dulating. The ones we experienced were quite definitely undulating and I remember being woken up thinking there was someone under my bed lifting up my mattress on their back. We did, of course, experience tremors almost all the time in Chile. I had only just arrived in the embassy and went into the registry to pick up some papers when someone shouted, 'Sit down, we're going to have an earthquake.' All those sitting down felt the tremors first – I hadn't because I was standing.

I had a marvellous trip with an ex-WRNS friend whose parents had a large farm down south in Chile. She drove me from Santiago into the wilds in her little truck, which she used for farm work from time to time. All the roads seemed to have huge cracks down the centre where they had just opened up during recent quakes. Presumably, if you happened to be there at the time you were just swallowed up. Quite terrifying. However, we had other problems to contend with when my friend's truck broke down and, as there were no mobiles in those days, we had to wait for someone to turn up and ask them to send help. This they did, and we eventually managed to get a lift into the nearest town and completed our journey by horse and carriage sent by the friends we were going to visit. It was like living in another age.

The house we visited was very big and rambling – masses of rooms leading through one another. They even had their own private chapel. All the walls were papered with posters of various kinds to cover the numerous cracks in the walls caused by earthquakes. It simply wasn't worth paying to have them repaired as the same thing would happen again quite soon. It is amazing how people learn to live with such disruption.

In 1969 I was posted to Malta, which was wonderful and only a few hours' flying time from the UK. Quite a change for me.

While I was there, my father and stepmother came out and we celebrated his 85th birthday. One day I took him somewhere which appealed to his archaeological interests. My stepmother was a keen artist, so she was happy to see us go off for the day while she got down to her painting. We joined a

small party of tourists who had a guide explaining things to them – then he said, 'The
next place we are going is into the dungeons.'
I thought to myself we are definitely not
going down there, but before I could say
anything I saw my father disappearing down
the ladder and I, of course, had to follow. Not
everyone went down, I have to say. After
some time the guide pointed out some hiero-
glyphics on the wall which had been written
hundreds of years ago by the prisoners held
there. Now I cannot tell you what the writing
was, but whatever it was my father was able
to read it. I know when I was about seven or
eight years of age a rabbi used to come to the
rectory to give him lessons in Hebrew, and I
know that he had studied Greek at some
stage. Frankly, it amazed me that at 85 he
could remember those sort of things. My
main problem at that time was how was he
going to climb up the ladder. I need not have
worried in the least – he managed very well
indeed and was none the worse.

In Malta I spent a lot of time in the local

mortuary. I had never been in one before. Mostly the job was identifying bodies from their passports and that sort of thing. I have never come across such a variety of problems and tragedies as we had to deal with there from time to time.

There were lighter moments too – as liquor was cheap and readily available, this attracted quite a number of alcoholics who eventually ended up in the local home for that sort of problem. Every now and then I, or my colleague, would be sent for to go and give advice, or just to let them know we were aware of their existence. On one occasion I received such a call to go and visit a lady who had ended up in that particular place. I was shown in – doors were locked behind me at every hand's turn – and eventually I found the lady in question. We had a very animated conversation and I got the gist of what was required – she wanted me to get her out into the wide world again as quickly as possible. I explained I could not do that, and moved on to another lady in much the same position. Suddenly I heard a loud clear voice from across the room saying, 'She's useless – from the British High Commission. No use at all.' I was left in no doubt whatsoever of her opinion of me and my capabilities. I had to laugh, I must say; most people were usually slightly more subtle about what they thought of us.

Sometimes the cases were really heartbreaking, like the young girl and her six-month-old baby son who had come out to Malta for a holiday with a young friend and her two-year-old child. On this occasion they separated, and the one with the six-month-old child came home to their rented house, bathed the baby and put him to bed in his cot and decided to take a bath herself. Tragically, the gas water-heater was faulty and she was eventually found dead a few hours later. The baby was taken into care and, to cut a long story short, I had to go to court to get him (a British subject) back. I ended up in a local convent with the Superintendent of Police and took possession of the baby and drove through the streets with flashing blue lights leading the way. Quite exciting! I often think I would like to find that young man and tell him the story, which he probably knows nothing or perhaps very little about.

Some people had never been out of the UK before coming to Malta and ended up in the most awful predicaments. One man fell through a plate-glass window on his first night on holiday. He severed an artery and bled to death before anything could be done for him. I was called in at 7 a.m. to deal with the situation. The same thing happened to a party of girl students who had come out to celebrate the end of their exams. They arranged always to be in by midnight, but on their first night one of the party went off with a local lad in a nice open-roofed sports car and by midnight there was no sign of her. The others waited up all night until 5 a.m. when the police came to inform them that she had been killed driving the fellow's car. You can imagine the state they were in by the time I reached them a couple of hours later. What a tragic holiday for them.

On one occasion I came very close to being blown up while driving home one Sunday morning after attending Morning Service at the cathedral in Valetta, where I sang in the choir. I lived in Marsa Xloqq, a small fishing village in the south of the island about seven miles out of Valetta. As I drove into the open countryside on a beautiful clear sunny day, there was a terrific explosion. My car, a Hill-man Imp, was literally lifted off the ground and I almost lost complete control of it. People started running from a nearby village in the direction of a black plume of smoke rising into the air. I got out of my car and found out from passers-by that it was a fireworks factory that had gone up. All the villages in Malta celebrate their patronal festivals with tremendous firework displays costing hundreds of pounds. These are often homemade by the locals in small huts or factories dotted around the countryside. In this case only three men were killed, but it could have been worse and I could easily have been included in the death toll. A few minutes earlier and I would have gone up in smoke too. When I arrived home approximately five miles away one could still smell the cordite quite distinctly.

I did three years in Malta and found great variety in my job, to say the least. Time never hung heavily on my hands, I can assure you. Nevertheless, it was on the whole a very enjoyable posting and I am still in touch with several of my Maltese colleagues.

9

A Trespass Forgiven

In 1972 I was posted to Singapore and arrived just in time for the Queen's visit on 18th February when she came to lay the foundation stone of the new High Commission in Tanglin Circus. En route I broke my journey in Teheran, where I had yet another friend at the embassy and managed to enjoy it all before things turned nasty.

Singapore was a wonderful posting. We had excellent accommodation, taken over from the Army who had then moved out – fully air-conditioned houses with lovely gardens just a short distance out of town. The place was changing rapidly and before I left, C.K. Tang in Orchard Road was about the only old building in that area and it was beginning to look like a mini New York with 40- and 50-storey buildings going up with revolving restaurants etc. Now I suppose they have been overtaken by much higher buildings. However, I do know that the famous Raffles Hotel still exists as I have just received a postcard of it from Michael and Susanne Breene (my nephew and his wife), who have been out there visiting their son David and his wife and family and have thoroughly enjoyed it.

One day a friend who had come out on relief duty from the UK asked me if I would like to join her and some friends for a visit to the islands off the east coast of Malaysia. Of course I was game for an expedition, so we set off in two cars – mine being one of them.

Having crossed over at Johor Bharu from Singapore into Malaysia and travelled for a couple of hours, we arrived at a fishing village where we left our cars and boarded a large fishing-boat. The locals sailed us out to our island and we arrived around midafternoon. The journey was extremely rough and I was not sick but feeling distinctly off colour. We got ashore with our paraphernalia and at this stage I found a palm tree in the shade and put a large sun hat over my face, Mexican style, and went to sleep, leaving the others to get organised. I should point out that this island was uninhabited, or so we thought, and we were going to camp there for the night. I don't remember what it was called or even if it did have a name.

On surfacing from my siesta under the palm trees, I spotted a neat little house (on stilts, Malay-style) at the top of the beach with a boathouse underneath. I thought that would suit me very nicely, and as darkness fell and we had eaten our evening meal cooked on a camp fire, I took my bedding up on to the veranda and settled down into a deep sleep. The others seemed to have rolled themselves up in plastic sheeting down on the beach.

Around midnight I was awoken by the chug-chug-chugging of a motorboat coming out of the darkness, then a splash followed by a flashlight being passed all over my sleeping quarters and ending up on me. I imagined this was a murder on the mainland and they were disposing of the body well away from civilisation. This was followed by a lot of chattering and a small procession coming up the beach in my direction. I jumped up, took all my bedding and threw it over the balcony rails and quickly followed it downstairs. By this time my pals had unravelled themselves from their plastic sheeting and were huddled together, smoking cigarettes. I presumed they were thinking along the same lines as I was – murder on the mainland and disposal of the body etc.

The procession passed quite close to us, carrying all their goods and chattels. They must have heard us calling to each other at an earlier stage as they said good evening as they went by. At least we felt they were not marauding Indians or suchlike.

I slept the rest of the night on the beach near my friends and awoke about 5 a.m. on a lovely cool sunny morning. I decided forth-with to don my swimsuit and make for the sea, which looked gorgeous. As I walked down the beach where the others were still wrapped in their plastic sheeting, it was amusing to see where animals of all sorts had walked round and round these humps on the beach, trying to make out what sort of un-usual creatures had come ashore during the night.

As I lolled about in the sea I was shortly joined by a nice Chinese lady from the cottage where I had been trespassing the night before. We said good morning to each other and I felt this was the moment when I must apologise for being on their veranda at midnight. She was very nice about it and said I was not to worry at all. She said they lived in Singapore; her son-in-law was the Italian manager of the famous Raffles Hotel and they came up quite often to get away from the hustle and bustle. She wound up the conversation by saying, 'I am Lee Kuan Yew's auntie.' Well, I thought, that's one way of getting a quick transfer back to the UK. Lee Kuan Yew just happened to be the Prime Minister of Singapore at the time. Fortunately, no more was heard about it and I completed my final tour abroad with the FCO, returning home on promotion to Second Secretary in 1975. I discovered I had done so many unhealthy posts (which at that time counted double towards my pension rights) that I had unwittingly knocked three years off my retiring date, which was a very nice surprise. I retired in the summer of 1976.

While in Singapore I spent a holiday in Bali with a friend from our embassy in Jakarta (Indonesia).

The Balinese are very attractive, friendly, lovely people. Those who looked after my friend and me in the hotel made us welcome in their homes and made sure we enjoyed our time there. Every Balinese is either a dancer, a wood carver or an artist. This starts from childhood and it was wonderful to watch the really small children performing quite complicated dance routines. No Balinese can see a boring flat surface anywhere. The doors in our hotel were all intricately carved, and there is a lovely story about when a Swedish firm arrived in the capital, Denpasar, to install a new drainage system. They dug up the roads and cemented the mud walls and left them overnight to dry before inserting the drain-pipes. When they returned the following day, much to their surprise, they found the smooth cement surfaces had been intricately carved.

We made a trip up-country to the charming village of Ubud, which is the centre of Balinese painting and very fine wood carving. While we were there we saw preparations for a Balinese funeral. The body is placed in a sarcophagus in the shape of an animal, chosen according to the caste and sex of the deceased person – a bull for a man and a cow for a woman. The sarcophagus is filled and covered with a variety of offerings – old coins, silks and brocades etc., and the whole thing is then cremated. The ashes are later consigned to the sea at dusk. It is quite an amazing sight.

On the homeward journey we stopped off in Jogjakarta in West Java, a small village about halfway between Bali and Jakarta. We stayed in a hotel and I remember distinctly the never-to-be-forgotten breakfast we had – a hard-boiled egg rolling around on a plastic plate and a couple of tablespoons of confectioner's chocolate (like hundreds and thousands) sticking to everything. Can you imagine that first thing in the morning? I think we probably had a ghastly cup of coffee as well to go with it.

The reason for our stop-off there was to visit Borobudor, a massive Buddhist monument in central Java 42 miles northwest of Jogjakarta. It was constructed between AD 778 and 850, and was apparently neglected from the year AD 1000 and completely overgrown with vegetation until restored by the Dutch in 1907 or thereabouts. I see that since I was there a second restoration was completed in the 1980s.

It is the most amazing construction in that it is shaped like a pyramid and consists of terraces – the first five being square and the higher three round. Each terrace represents the stages towards perfection in an individual's life (Nirvana). The squares represent the earth and the rounds represent heaven. The Buddhist pilgrim is required to circumvent the monument nine times before reaching the top, where there are four stairways – one on each side – leading to the top. There are 72 huge bell-shaped memorial shrines (stupas) on the upper circular terraces containing meditative Buddhas.

A really fabulous monument and well worth a visit for anyone finding themselves in that part of the world.

I later made a second visit to Indonesia, this time to the island of Sumatra. Singapore Airlines were trying out some experimental flights to Medan to see if they could get enough people interested in the area to start up a regular flight there. The area we visited had been a hill station for the Dutch in the old days and had been allowed to become very run-down. I don't remember anything very outstanding about the trip except a village we visited at the far end of a large lake. The houses were on stilts and the families made us very welcome. The whole set-up was extremely primitive but attractive and it was funny in one house to see a very ancient Singer sewing machine, obviously still in use. It would have been a great advertisement, wouldn't it?

On one occasion we had a day on our own and we wondered what on earth we would do with ourselves. I heard someone saying you could have a massage, so I asked for further details. It really was great fun. A tiny little Indonesian lady about four foot tall arrived with her large bottle of home-made herbal lotion. My friend was quite a tall, well-made lady, so I suggested she went first for her massage. Everything seemed to be going quite well, but towards the end of her treatment I heard some high-pitched screams coming from her room and I must say I did have my doubts about what was happening to her. When my turn came around, I was somewhat apprehensive. All went well until the final touches were being put to me – and they fully explained my friend's screams. This tiny little lady walked up and down on my spine – you could hear the bones cracking as she did so. It was my turn to scream, although I have to say it didn't really hurt at all. It amused me no end when I thought of her size compared with my well-built five foot ten friend. This was followed by a quick dip in the lake, and I must say one really felt wonderful after it. History does not relate what was in the home-made lotion. I would love to know.

On my first midtour home leave from Singapore I managed to fit in a visit to the Seychelles and Kenya by taking the southern route via Kuala Lumpur and Colombo. The Seychelles in those days was only beginning to be talked about as a tourist attraction. I had met someone in Singapore who told me he was hoping to put the Seychelles on the tourist map and it sounded a very attractive place by all accounts. At that stage I think there was only one large hotel – however, I headed for The Fisherman's Cove, which was a really delightful small hotel just off the beach, where I spent a few days lolling about swimming and taking life easy. It was really idyllic.

Back in the FCO in London I met up with a colleague from my Haiti days and he told me he had just been posted to the Seychelles and was very much looking forward to such a wonderful posting. Sadly, some months later I read of his death from drowning shortly after his arrival there. He had been swimming with his daughter, who was out on holiday with them; she managed to get ashore but he was swept away. I was totally unaware of any danger of currents and spent most of my time in and out of the sea for the short time I was there. It was a great shock to hear of his death.

From the Seychelles I flew to Nairobi, where I had some friends at the High Commission. After a couple of days visiting them and getting the lie of the land, I kept an eye on the notice board in my hotel which outlined the various safaris setting off each day at the crack of dawn.

The first trip I did was to Treetops, a game-viewing hideaway in the Aberdare Forest. It was here in 1952 that Princess Elizabeth learned she had become Queen on the sudden death of her father George VI. The Treetops we visited, however, was not the one where all this took place – it had been burned down by the Mau Mau, a secret terrorist organisation intent on driving the white settlers out of Kenya. A new one had been constructed on the opposite side of the watering hole.

We were escorted from our transport by a hunter with his rifle cocked at the ready, and there were ladders strategically placed for us to make a quick escape in case of any unexpected arrivals from the forest.

Our first meal was tea on the rooftop, all beautifully laid out, with very smart waiters in white with red cummerbunds in attendance. At this stage we had to watch out for the arrival of the baboons, who would make a quick dash for the sandwiches and cakes, given half a chance. Dinner was served about 8 p.m. and afterwards we could watch animals arriving for their evening drinks and family get-togethers. The elephants were fantastic. They are very family-orientated, so their babies are very well protected by their relatives, and it was great fun to see the families meeting and greeting each other – lots of trunk-shaking, which I had never seen before.

Our rooms, which overlooked the drinking hole, were fitted with alarms to waken us if anything interesting happened during the night. Flood-lighting was switched on well before dark so that the animals were not worried by the sudden change. There was a great variety of animals coming to drink together and it was amusing to watch the little elephants seeing off the ones they didn't like, such as warthogs. They really made sure they chased them well away back into the forest.

On the return journey to Nairobi we stopped off in Nyeri, a hill-town on the slopes of the Aberdare Mountains, and had lunch at the famous Outspan Hotel, where Lord Baden-Powell, founder of the Boy Scout Movement, chose to retire to and where he spent the last years of his life. He is buried in the local churchyard there.

Back in Nairobi, I had booked to go on safari to the Amboseli Game Reserve, which lies not far from the foot of Mount Kilimanjaro. We set off the day after our return from Treetops early in the morning and drove south through Maasai Mara territory down as far as the border with Tanzania. It was a wonderful journey as we wended our way through the flocks of sheep and goats herded by the magnificent tall, erect, warrior-like Maasai tribesmen and their women in their deep rose-coloured robes. Even the women are well over six foot tall and decorated in their brightly coloured hand-made beaded jewellery. We made a couple of stops at some of the Maasai villages and mingled with the locals doing their daily shopping in the market, which was fascinating.

On arrival in Amboseli we were allocated our rooms, which were quite spartan but adequate. After tea we went off on a trip in an open-roofed Land Rover in which we were able to stand up and observe everything. Looking in the distance, we could see the snow-capped Mount Kilimanjaro and a herd of elephants on the move quite near us. Giraffes and their families were continually crossing in front of us and even stopping and staring at us. We spent most of the next day just driving around the reserve, finding animals tucked away in the shade at midday and later on when it was cooler strolling out for a drink or to hunt for food.

One night I was awoken by a noise outside my room – I just hoped it was not a herd of elephants preparing to knock my door down. Fortunately, it was nothing like that at all, only a zebra and her baby eating the flowers in my little garden. I didn't mind in the least and they continued to enjoy themselves – probably until the dawn came up and they had run out of flowers.

I thought Kenya was a really fabulous country and I would have loved to have had a posting there, but it wasn't to be and in any case I was on my last tour before retiring.

10

A Mysterious Disappearance – and Other Travellers' Tales

Back in Singapore for a second tour, I managed to see a bit more of Malaysia, which I loved. On one occasion I was due for a long weekend off and a friend recommended a trip up to Fraser's Hill, a hill-station outside Kuala Lumpur. It was an easy train journey and the railways owned some nice bungalows there for short breaks from KL and Singapore. I therefore booked one, and arrived in KL. I was met by a friend stationed there and invited to a curry lunch with six or eight other friends from the High Commission. A good time was had by all and later we made our way to the railway station where I was to board my train for the short trip to Fraser's Hill. Some helpful pal (having had a few drinks too many, I suspect) had written down on my timetable the name of the wrong station for me to get off. He had in fact written down the station for the Cameron Highlands, much further away.

I arrived quite late on in the evening (between 6 and 7 p.m.), only to discover I had just missed the train back to Fraser's Hill. I therefore had to get myself to the Cameron Highlands, the first part of which I did in a taxi laden with livestock in the back. The driver took me as far as a small town called Tapah where the highway begins to climb steeply up to the highlands; there he found a friendly Tamil who volunteered to drive me the remaining 35 miles in his comfortable Mercedes, which was just as well as it was several hours' journey through dense jungle and an extremely dangerous road.

During the journey I turned down the windows to enjoy the jungle sounds, and from time to time by the light of our head-lamps I could see small figures running back and forth. I also occasionally got a glimpse into the odd hut with people sitting round an oil lamp. It occurred to me at that stage that it was dangerous to allow children out in the dark in the jungle.

We arrived at the Camerons around 9 p.m. and I instructed the driver to take me to the only hotel I knew of in the area, called the Smoke House. Of course it was full up, but I said, 'I'll just sit here in a comfortable chair,' as I had no intention of going else-where at that time of night. Eventually the receptionist realised I was not moving on, so she called the manager, an ex-serviceman, Stan Smith, who ran the hotel with his Chinese wife. The result was I ended up with the honeymoon suite – a delightful room with a huge four-poster bed complete with ladder to climb into it. I was most grateful, I can tell you, to have such wonder-ful accommodation.

When I woke the next morning I took

myself for a walk before breakfast and discovered the hotel was just like something you would find in the stockbroker belt in the heart of Surrey – situated on the edge of a golf course and surrounded by flowers of all kinds. A really delightful place. As I walked along the road I noticed signs saying 'Jungle walk No. 1', 'Jungle walk No. 2' etc., so I decided to go down one and wander along. Eventually I came to a small Anglican church. I noted the time of service and decided to go back to the hotel for breakfast and return for the 10.30 a.m. service, which I did. As I walked in, the vicar was announcing the first hymn and I knew instantly where he came from – believe it or not, he was from Londonderry, Northern Ireland.

After returning to the hotel, Stan, the manager of the hotel, joined me and we chatted for a while. He asked me how I was getting back to Singapore from there and I replied that I had no idea. He said, 'I'll take you as far as KL this afternoon, if you like.' I was delighted and was amazed when he turned up at the entrance of the hotel in a gorgeous beige-coloured Bentley. It was just like sitting in a really comfortable armchair.

'What would happen if we shot off the road and down into the jungle here?' I asked Stan as we drove down the very steep winding road from the Cameron Highlands en route to KL on my return journey to Singapore. Incidentally, the Cameron Highlands had first been mapped a hundred years ago by a Scottish surveyor called Cameron and has been a popular hill station for people working in KL and Singapore ever since. My friend replied, 'Oh, we'd be found quite soon, probably by the *orang asli*, the forest tribesmen, who hunt here with their blowpipes at night and know every inch of the jungle.' These, of course, were the 'children' I thought were out playing in the jungle after dark!

The reason I asked this question was because I was comparing it with driving in a similar situation in Bolivia. There one knew there was not the slightest hope of recovery if your car went off the narrow roads and down into the dense jungle. Small wooden crosses at the roadside every mile or so indicated where trucks and cars had gone over either accidentally or on purpose. In fact, it was purported to be a favourite way of getting rid of politicians and the like with the absolute certainty they would not return. Either that method or falling out of a helicopter seemed to be in vogue at that time. Travelling with a local driver was a hazardous business there as he would frequently take his hands off the driving wheel to cross himself at every wayside sign indicating where a tragedy had occurred. However, back to Malaysia.

Another question I had to ask Stan was, 'Do people ever disappear up here in the jungle?'

'Well,' he said, 'not very often. We do have tigers wandering across the golf course at night from time to time, which can be dangerous. But of course there was the case of Jim Thompson.'

'Oh,' I said, 'you mean the American who helped the Thai silk industry get off the ground and become famous in the 1950s and 60s?'

'Yes,' he replied. 'Jim disappeared up here.'

I was amazed. I had read about Jim's disappearance in *Time* magazine while I was in Haiti, but I thought it was in Thailand he had gone missing. I was interested as I had bought my Thai silk from Jim in his shop in Bangkok. He had actually attended to me, helped me choose my material, and he was a very nice friendly person in his early sixties when he went missing.

Jim's story is a very strange one indeed and has been described as 'an enduring mystery'. He had come up from Singapore to the Cameron Highlands to spend Easter (1967) weekend with Dr T.G. Ling and his American wife Helen, who had a very nice antiques shop in Singapore where I bought several Chinese snuff bottles to add to my collection. After attending Easter Sunday Morning

Service at the local Anglican church, they drove into the foothills of the Highlands to have a picnic lunch. Jim had apparently suddenly changed his mind about going at the last moment for some unknown reason, but he was eventually persuaded to join them. Soon after they all returned home to the Lings' cottage, everyone went to their rooms for a siesta.

Later that evening my friend Stan (manager of the Smoke House) was in the bar of the hotel drinking with some local pals. Someone had seen or heard that Jim Thompson was in the area for the weekend and wondered why he had not turned up for a drink and a chat. Stan phoned the Lings to ask where Jim was. They said he was not around, but while they were having their siesta they heard what they thought was Jim walking past their window on the gravel path. They presumed he had gone down to see his friends in the Smoke House bar.

Four hundred British jungle-trained Gurkhas were called in and searched the area very thoroughly, but no trace of Jim was ever found – not even a footprint or traces of a body being dragged away by a tiger or an item of clothing – no clue whatsoever was found to explain what became of him. The fact that he was possibly a member of the CIA may have had something to do with it. Some time later on, his sister was murdered in America, but no connection could be made there either. It just remains a mystery to this day.

I am going to produce here some hints I was given while up in the Cameron Highlands which may come in useful to other people who may be travelling in jungle areas. I only received these after I had wandered about on the jungle paths without a thought of any danger.

Hints for walkers in the Malaysian or other jungle

1. Never walk alone.

2. Inform a friend before leaving of:
   a) Route you intend to take
   b) Your expected time of return

3. If you are lost, walk either due East or West (i.e. in the opposite direction to that which you left the main road) until you meet the main road again.

4. If you are uncertain as to the direction of East or West, remain stationary, if possible near a stream until you are found. It may take 24 hours to find you.

DO NOT PANIC

5. You should always take the following items on your walk:
   a) A filled water bottle
   b) A compass
   c) A whistle
   d) A torch
   e) A little food (e.g. chocolate)
   f) A knife
   g) A box of matches

6. You should always wear long trousers and

long sleeves. This will protect you from being scratched and will keep you warm at night.

7. KEEP TO THE NUMBERED PATHS AS SHOWN ON YOUR MAP IF YOU HAVE ONE.

Talking of 'honeymoon suites' reminded me of a trip I made from Rio de Janeiro to Dakar (West Africa) on my journey home from South America. It was an overnight flight and was very bumpy indeed, so I was quite glad when we eventually arrived in Dakar and got through Customs quite quickly and boarded the bus which would take us into the city. To my horror, at the first stop everyone got off the bus and I was the sole passenger for the rest of the journey. We drove in pitch darkness for about 30 minutes, though it seemed much longer to me. At last I began to see lights which indicated we were coming into civilisation and I was dropped off at my hotel in the centre of town. It was then about 2 a.m. and I was looking forward to getting to bed as quickly as possible.

On arrival inside the hotel there was no sign of life at all. I rang a bell and, as if by magic, a head appeared from under the reception desk and his first welcoming words were, 'I buy your radio.' I was carrying a small transistor which he quite fancied. I asked to be shown to my room, which had been booked some months before, but regrettably there were no rooms available. However, they said I could, as a special concession, have the 'honeymoon suite'. I had another word for it actually. The mattress was corrugated and madly uncomfortable. I spent the night pushing items of furniture up against the door to keep out intruders, so next morning I left at the first opportunity and made for the Canary Islands, where I spent a few days recuperating, and flew on to Lisbon, where I had a friend at the embassy, and thence to the UK.

During my years of travelling I made several

attempts to get to Katmandu – all unsuccessful. In fact at one stage I was offered a posting there but could not take up the offer at the time. At last an opportunity arose on my final trip home from Singapore. I managed to pick up a Nepalese Airline flight at Calcutta and arrived in Katmandu, where I had a friend at the embassy. I had mentioned to her that I was very interested in Tiger Tops, which I had read about but as things turned out it was not possible.

Sadly, on 31st May 1975, just before I arrived in Nepal, Sir Edmund Hillary's wife Louise and their 16-year-old daughter Belinda were killed in Katmandu as their plane took off on the last lap of their journey up to their home in the mountains, and crashed on the runway, killing everyone on board. Lady Hillary had gone down to Delhi to pick up Belinda for the school holidays.

My friend, who was the Vice Consul, was involved in helping with the whole situation and organising the funeral. They were cremated at the 'burning ghats' outside

Katmandu at Sir Edmund's request.

As a result of this, my friend said, 'Instead of Tiger Tops, I have arranged for us to fly round Everest before breakfast on Thursday at five a.m.', and that is exactly what we did on a most beautiful clear day – and we have certificates to prove it!

Tiger Tops in the Chitwan National Park is in the Terai, a low-lying area of Nepal, a 30 minute flight south of Katmandu. It consists of forests, jungles, world-famous hunting grounds and the elusive Royal Bengal Tigers. Accommodation is available at the Temple Tiger Jungle Lodge which you can do nowadays by four-wheel drive vehicle, but back in the 70s it was a two hour elephant ride from the airport. I expect my friend was quite relieved she didn't have to accompany me on that jaunt. At one stage a river had to be crossed and I heard it described as akin to 'floating on a cork in the middle of the Atlantic'; I'm glad we flew round Everest instead.

Writing this reminded me of sitting in

church in Baghdad in June 1953, attending a special service to commemorate the coronation of Queen Elizabeth II, when someone tapped me on the shoulder and said, 'Hillary has climbed Everest.' He and Sherpa Tensing had reached the summit and, of course, there was great excitement and celebrations. Actually, I believe they had reached the summit a few days earlier but the announcement had been withheld to coincide with Coronation Day.

Katmandu was such a wonderful, colourful and peaceful place it was a terrible shock to hear of the tragic death of nine of the Nepalese royal family at the hands of the Eton-educated Crown Prince Dipendra on 1st June 2001. It was brought about because of his love affair with a girl who was unacceptable to the senior members of the royal family. It is really hard to believe such shocking events take place from time to time and we so quickly forget them. It brings to mind the appalling case of the young King Feisal II of Iraq and 30 members of his family who were completely wiped out in a *coup d'état* in 1958. The difference in the two events is, of course, the Nepalese tragedy was self-inflicted by a member of their own family, which made it even more difficult to comprehend.

Sir Edmund Hillary, who was appointed High Commissioner for New Zealand in India in 1985, said recently that he was extremely concerned about the current situation there. The monarchy, with a completely new royal family, and the present government are under enormous pressure and in danger of being overthrown by a Maoist element. What a tragedy!

A week or so ago I opened my daily newspaper and there in front of me was a picture of the R.101 airship, which brought back childhood memories of 1930. I had gone out after supper with my father and our fox terrier for a walk round the garden. It was a beautiful clear moonlit night. As we strolled on the lawn the dog stood up on his hind legs, barked and barked up at the sky and behaved in a very odd way. We laughed and wondered what was wrong with him. Then we followed his gaze into the sky and there silently (to us) was the R.101 passing over in the moonlight on its maiden voyage. It was a really beautiful sight. We heard nothing, but the dog did!

Next morning we learnt it had crashed in Northern France. That put an end to any further development of the airship as far as the British were concerned. They were just too dangerous. There was an R.100 but I understand it was withdrawn and dismantled. The Germans continued to produce airships until the awful disaster in 1937 when the *Hindenburg* burst into flames while coming in to land in New York and almost everyone on board was killed.

While we are on the subject of air travel I want to record that in 1991 an ex-WRNS friend and I flew out to Egypt on Concorde. We went through the sound barrier over the Mediterranean near Sardinia and it seemed just like a rather bad gear change to us – nothing spectacular at all. One thing we didn't care for much was the flight details displayed for everyone to see – I'd rather not know that we are hurtling down the runway at 250 miles an hour or whatever speed they do on take off. Also we were amazed at how narrow the central gangway and the seats were. Fortunately, we are both fairly small so space didn't bother us, but we did wonder how a six-foot man would manage in such cramped conditions. However, we did very much enjoy the food which we consumed for most of the journey to Cairo.

Another dreadful shock we had on 25th July 2000 was when a friend and I were returning home from Eastbourne, East Sussex, where we had spent the day. We broke our journey to have a cup of tea at a restaurant where they had a large television on the wall. As we watched, it showed the appalling pictures of Concorde crashing in Paris – we could not believe it. It apparently hit an object on the runway which caused damage to the fuel tanks. One hundred and thirteen people perished in this terrible disaster. It was 7th November 2001 before Concorde was back in service again.

Sadly, on 24th October 2003, British Airways Concorde made its last flight across the Atlantic and our entire fleet of seven were withdrawn from service. They will be dispersed to various parts of the globe where they can be studied and admired by future generations of enthusiasts. The French had already withdrawn their fleet on 31st May 2003.

The last few years since the Paris catastrophe, followed by the 9/11 terrorist attacks in 2001 in New York, had had a devastating effect on Concorde's financial situation. Almost 40 company chairmen and chief executives who regularly flew the Atlantic with them were killed, robbing them of passengers at a crucial time when they were just beginning to recover.

All I can add is, 'Well done – good and faithful servant!' There will never be another like her – in our time at least and probably not for many years to come.

Finally, and on a happier theme, I want to record that after my retirement I still continued to travel for several years. I visited cousins in Toronto and my god-daughter in Calgary and took a trip through the Rockies to Vancouver. That is a place I would love to have found earlier in my youth. Vancouver Island is a delightful spot – no wonder so many of our Officers of senior rank retire there. I believe it never has anything more than a heavy frost in winter. Sounds OK to me! I also visited my god-daughter Patricia with her mother (an old school friend) when she was living in Houston, Texas. The important item to be recorded at this point is that I had my one and only flying lesson in Houston. I was chatting to John, Patricia's husband at that time, and I casually said I always regretted not having taken flying lessons in my younger days. The next thing I knew I was in a small Cessna plane at the local airfield having a lesson. I think Patricia and her mother were quite apprehensive until John and I returned home a couple of hours later. It was good fun, however, and I have photographs to prove it, but sadly no certificate of proficiency.

The publishers hope that this book has given you enjoyable reading. Large Print Books are especially designed to be as easy to see and hold as possible. If you wish a complete list of our books please ask at your local library or write directly to:

Dales Large Print Books
Magna House, Long Preston,
Skipton, North Yorkshire.
BD23 4ND